Capitalism

FOR BEGINNERS

ADAM SMITH

KARL MARX

WERNER SOMBART

J.M. KEYNES

MILTON FRIEDMAN

by
Robert Lekachman
& Borin Van Loon

Pantheon Books, New York

Text Copyright © 1981 by Robert Lekachman

Illustrations Copyright © 1981 by Borin Van Loon

Library of Congress Cataloging in Publication Data

Lekachman, Robert.
  Capitalism for beginners.

  Bibliography: p.
  1. Capitalism. 2. Economics. 3. Economic
history—1945—   . 4. United States—Economic
history—1971—   . I. Title.
HB501.L3135   330.12′2   80-8648
ISBN 0-394-51027-5   AACR2
ISBN 0-394-73863-2 (pbk.)

Manufactured in the United States of America
98765432

About the author and illustrator

Robert Lekachman, born in New York in 1920, received his B.A.
and Ph. D. from Columbia University.

Mr. Lekachman has written for *The New York Times Book Review,
The Atlantic Monthly, Harpers*, *The New York Review of Books,
The New Republic,* and *The Nation.* He is the author of *A History of
Economic Ideas* and *The Age of Keynes,* and has edited five col-
lections of writings on the subject of economics. He was a Rockefeller Fellow in 1962–3, and is now chairman of the economics
department at the University of New York, Stony Brook.

Borin Van Loon is an illustrator living in Great Britain.

What Is Capitalism?

The bare, basic essentials of capitalism are these:

1. Capital is the portion of a nation's wealth that is **man-made** and therefore **reproducible**.

2. Under capitalism, a society's capital equipment, its means of production, is owned by a minority of individuals who have the legal right to use this property for private gain.

3. Capitalism relies on the market system, which determines distribution, allocates resources and establishes the income levels, wages, rents and profits of the different social classes.

There's more to capitalism than that. It can refer to an economic system, the society built on it and a historical stage of Western, or First World, civilization.

Few analysts of capitalism have ever thought the system was permanent. Some rejoice at its certain demise. Others express regret. The trouble is, can we trust any economist to tell us the truth about capitalism? Capitalism has continually suffered, and overcome, crisis. And today, after a long post-war period of affluence, the world economy faces a new recession. Is there anything new about this crisis? Yes, since according to our policy-makers, it should never have happened! Rising unemployment and inflationary price levels really worry them. Inflation contributes to the instability of financial markets, trade imbalances and the fiscal crisis of the state. The spread of uncertainty and instability has undermined political cohesion and the reputation of governments for successful economic management.

GALLOPING INFLA

UNEMPLOYMENT

I f you liked this book and would like to pass a copy on to someone else, please check with your local bookstore, online bookseller, or use this form:

Name _____

Address _____

City _____State _____ Zip _____

Payment by: ☐ Check   ☐ Credit Card

Credit Card Number: _____

Expiration Date: _____

Check which: ☐ MasterCard   ☐ Visa

A Hawaiian Life _____ copies @ $14.95 each $ _____

California residents, please add applicable sales tax $ _____

Shipping: $3.20/first copy; $1.60 each additional copy* $ _____

Total enclosed, or charge my credit card (above) $ _____

For more than 5 copies, please contact the publisher for quantity rates. Send completed order form and your credit card information, check, or money order to:

Kealia Press
Order Department
P.O. Box 12804
Lahaina, HI 96761
Telephone Orders: 1-888-710-1100 (toll free)

or order via our Web Site at www.kealiapress.com

*International shipping is extra. Please contact us for the shipping rates to your location, if outside the United States.

Is this the end for capitalism?

Waiting For Capitalism To Fall...

Karl Marx did predict an end to capitalism in Volume One of his monumental work, **Capital**.

....is like waiting for Switzerland to turn Communist!

Along with the constantly diminishing number of magnates of capital, who usurp and monopolize all advantages of this process of transformation, grows the mass of misery, oppression, slavery, degradation, exploitation; but with this too grows the revolt of the working class, a class always increasing in number, and disciplined, united, organized by the very mechanism of the process of capitalist production itself. The monopoly of capital becomes a fetter upon the mode of production which has sprung up and flourished with it and under it. Centralization of the means of production and the socialization of labour at last reach a point where they become incompatible with their capitalist integument. This integument is burst asunder. The knell of capitalist private property sounds. The expropriators are expropriated.

Always a prudent prophet, Marx refrained from dating capitalism's demise. Just as well. The beast has turned out to be tougher, craftier and more durable than the more optimistic of Marx's disciples expected. All the same, Marx emphasized a crucial point in asserting that steady growth and expansion were vital to capitalism's health.

A TOUGH OLD RHINO...

Capitalism may survive – but does it have a future?

The world economy is held together by elastic bands. Vast sums of money churn around in banks and security exchanges — billions of dollars and other currencies flow from rich countries and poor lands without oil to OPEC. Billions return from OPEC to European and American banks. More billions are loaned by these banks to developing societies in Africa, Latin America and Asia so that they can pay their oil bills.

Can the operators of its financial
and commercial mechanisms
restore prosperity and price
stability by fiddling with money
supplies, interest rates, taxes and
government spending?
Japan and Germany are faring
quite well, but the leader of the
capitalist world, the United
States, suffers from acute
inflation, persistent
unemployment, declining
productivity, huge balance of
payments deficits (Americans are
buying a lot more from the rest of
the world than the rest of the world
cares to buy from American
exporters), and political
incapacity to cope with any of
these maladies.

In the U.S., fortress of capitalism,
many conservatives look upon
Europe's several mild, 'welfare
state' governments as being
dangerously socialist.
Which raises an interesting
question . . .

9

Why Is There No Socialism In The U.S.A.?

One answer, circa 1892, came from Friedrich Engels, Karl Marx's partner. He repeated what Alexis de Tocqueville had already written in the 1830s.

In no other country of the world is the love of property keener or more alert than in the United States, and nowhere else does the majority display less inclination towards doctrines which in any way threaten the way property is owned.

It is remarkable how firmly rooted are bourgeois prejudices even in the working class in such a young country.

It was a society without class consciousness. A worker seemed to have every opportunity to become independent, to rise **from** his class rather than **with** it. Besides, there was a frontier, plenty of free land to develop.

Yet Engels expected the rise of socialism. One day the frontier would close and self-employed independence would be turned into wage labour.

In fact, for a time, The Socialist Party of America, founded in 1901, seemed pretty impressive. But even at its best, in 1912, the Party's leader, Eugene Debs, only got 6% of the popular vote. After this, it began to fade.

DEBS FAILS TO GET VOTES

DECLINE IMMINENT

Why did socialism fail to catch on – even during the Great Depression?

In 1904 the German economic historian Werner Sombart, at that time a socialist sympathizer (later a Nazi sympathizer) visited the U.S. His 1906 classic, **Why Is There No Socialism in the United States?** gave another memorable answer.

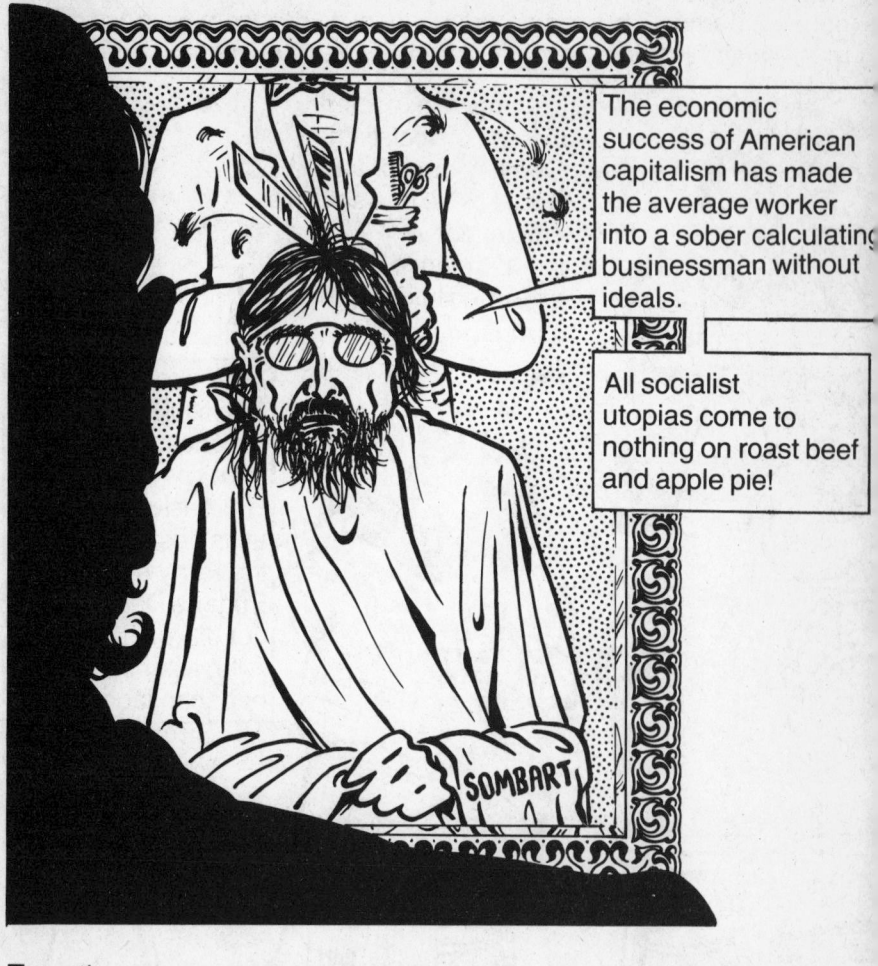

The economic success of American capitalism has made the average worker into a sober calculating businessman without ideals.

All socialist utopias come to nothing on roast beef and apple pie!

SOMBART

True, the average American worker enjoyed a higher standard of living than his European counterpart. But is it true that affluence undermines the spread of socialism? That radicalism and prosperity don't mix? Not necessarily. Socialist activity doesn't always decline among increasingly prosperous workers. And socialism often finds its greatest support among the highest paid, skilled workers. So 'affluence' is only part of the answer.

12

The prospects for moving out of his class are undoubtedly greater for the worker in America than in old Europe.

America is famous for its rags-to-riches stories. But how many Carnegies are there? The self-made man is largely a myth. 3 in 10 sons of blue collar workers will make it to white collar status. But only 1 in 10 will achieve longer-range mobility.

Vertical or upward status mobility is less important than horizontal or geographical mobility.

Americans are restless seekers after old and new frontiers. In many communities, populations are constantly changing, and this helps to undermine the establishment of socialism. It is hard to build up a collective working-class attitude in an atmosphere of individual restlessness.

Improvement remains a question of individual self-advancement rather than collective action.

...OVER MY DEAD BODY...

SOMBART

In America, a worker doesn't have to "bow and scrape" as he does in Europe. Daily life is more democratic.

There is respect for all honest work — less for leisure.

Sombart observed that the United States was "born Bourgeois". It didn't inherit any of Europe's pre-capitalist social groupings – peasants, artisans or aristocrats. The U.S., more than any country, enshrines the individual aim of owning property. It is hard to grow socialism in that soil!

Workers in America never had to struggle for elementary political rights, which was more than half the battle for European workers. The ballot and basic rights of citizenship were free gifts which preceded the birth of the American labour movement. Lack of interest in socialism was partly explained by this unusual relationship to the state — by the workers' unusually strong faith in the existing political system.

And that helps to explain the special relationship between capital and labour.

You bet it does!

GOMPERS

In 1901, the year of the Socialist Party's foundation, the AFL (American Federation of Labor) rejected the idea of an independent working-class party and instead opted for bread and butter gains. Samuel Gompers, president of the AFL from 1886 to 1924, when asked what labour wanted, responded MORE!

IMMIGRATION

The huge numbers of immigrants to America had the effect of splintering wage earners into mutually suspicious nationality groups.

Remember too, many immigrants did not intend to settle — just to make money and return home. (For instance, between 1907-11, for every 100 Italians landed in the U.S., 73 returned to Italy.) As for socialism . . .

Bad enough to be a Kike or a Dago — no need to be called a Red too!

The Anatomy Of Capitalism

American capitalism, on the surface, seems all practical business and no fancy theories. But its roots go deep. Back in the 19th century, when the US was the world's only political democracy, liberty itself and the "innate rights of man" were identified with the rise of free market capitalism. What has become a faith was once a theory, first proposed by a Scottish economist, Adam Smith (1723-

SMIFF

MILT

90) in that crucial year 1776. What he described as the ideal of free enterprise and the utopia of self-interest still animates conventional economics today.

The uniform, constant and uninterrupted effort of every man, to better his own condition, the principle from which national and public as well as private opulence is originally derived, is frequently powerful enough to maintain the natural progress of things towards improvement, in spite both of the extravagance of government, and of the greatest errors of administration.

And here's Milton Friedman in 1980.

Adam Smith's flash of genius was his recognition that the prices that emerged from voluntary transactions between buyers and sellers — for short, in a free market — could coordinate the activity of millions of people, each seeking his own interest, in such a way as to make everyone better off. It was a startling idea then, and it remains one today, that economic order can emerge as the unintended consequence of the actions of many people, each seeking his own interest.

Smith and his modern disciple Friedman are describing Libertyville: an ideal, free market economy; a capitalist utopia. Let's see what they consider the minimum conditions of a free market to be.

19

Libertyville: The Free Market

Very large numbers of sellers, none of them in control of a significant fraction of their market, compete furiously to win favour with even larger numbers of buyers, most of them individual consumers and the remainder other businessmen.

Prices are gloriously impersonal.

Prudent shoppers switch to pork when beef prices escalate, limes when lemons become expensive, margarine when butter costs too much and so on.

1. SELLERS, BUYERS & THE PRICE SYSTEM

The price system is the arena of self-interest. For sellers, it takes the shape of profit maximization; for consumers, maximization of the satisfaction they derive from rational choice of the things they buy. All parties respond to market signals. Sellers enlarge output when prices rise and reduce it as they decline. Buyers shift in opposite directions, purchasing more as prices diminish and less as they increase.

When labour becomes scarce and expensive, employers substitute machines.

The price system is wonderfully democratic, the least elitist of human arrangements. Led Zeppelin makes more money for its performances than the Guarneri Quartet because more people eagerly buy tickets and records to hear the first group than the second. In free markets, the ringing of cash registers measures better and worse, not your superior taste or mine.

Free markets educate all parties. Businessmen who offer low-quality products in short order lose customers to rivals. If the former learn from this experience, they correct mistakes, improve

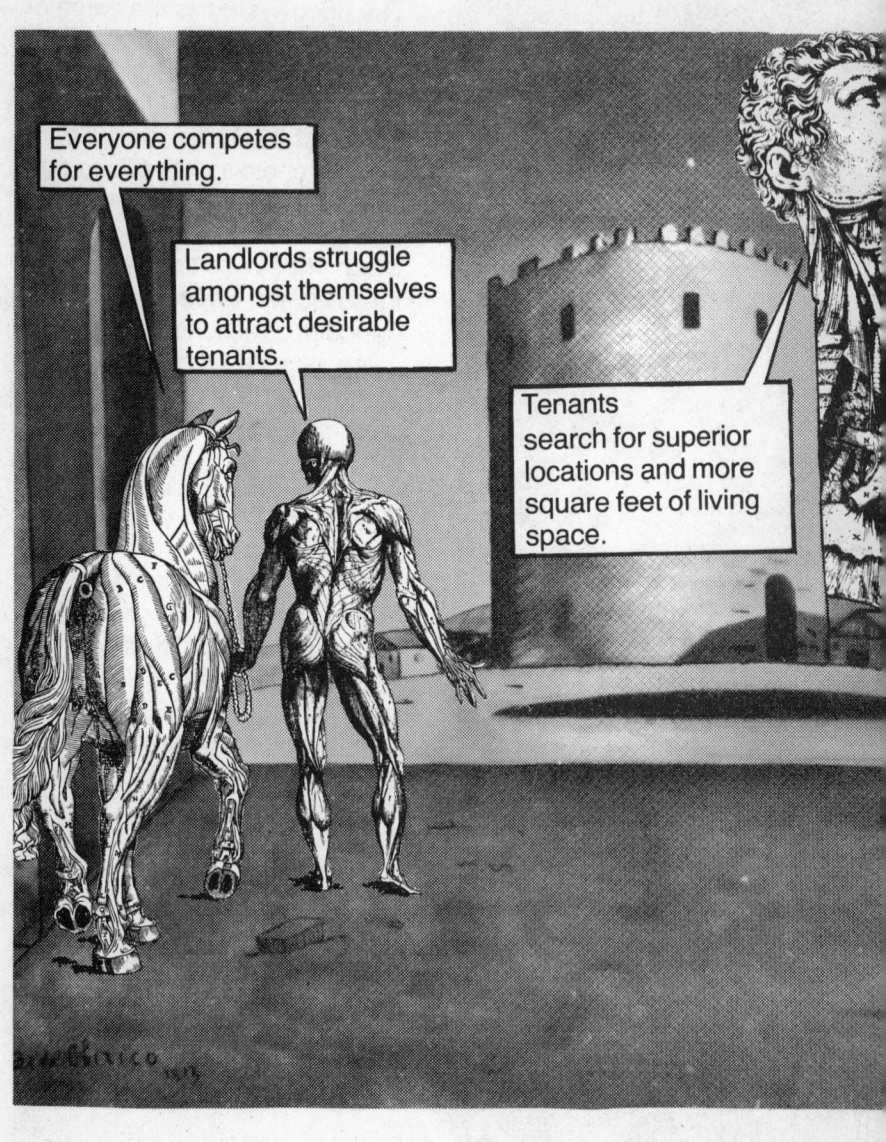

Everyone competes for everything.

Landlords struggle amongst themselves to attract desirable tenants.

Tenants search for superior locations and more square feet of living space.

quality, regain customers and survive. Businessmen who are too stupid or slothful to benefit from their own blunders perish.

Slow-witted or inattentive customers, similarly, realize from painful experience that they have wasted precious money on the wrong merchandise or even the right merchandise in the wrong quantities.

Sellers don't **want** to furnish reliable merchandise of good quality. Their aspiration is profit. It is the buyers who seek good products at low prices. If in the end free markets compel sellers to meet the expectations of buyers, it is because competition exerts unremitting pressure upon each seller to keep prices low and quality high out of fear that otherwise his rivals will steal his customers.

The moral for businessmen is stark: the way to enlarge profit is to operate more efficiently and meet more completely the wishes of the customers. Even then the extra earnings are temporary, because jealous rivals quickly emulate the tactics of creative innovators.

rifty savers
st about for the
ghest possible
es of bank interest.

Banks compete among themselves to lure depositors.

Laissez-faire simply means "letting things be", no regulation, no interference.

In competitive markets, no one sets prices. On the Paris Bourse, quotations for most securities traded will be at the end of a day's trading different from at the day's beginning, entirely as a consequence of the offers made

No clumsy bureaucrat in a government office or the headquarters of a private monopoly dictates the price of anything.

If you or I rebel against the price of coffee or claret, we are free drink less of either beverage or switc tea and vin ordina by buyers and the prices asked by sellers. Traders on both sides of

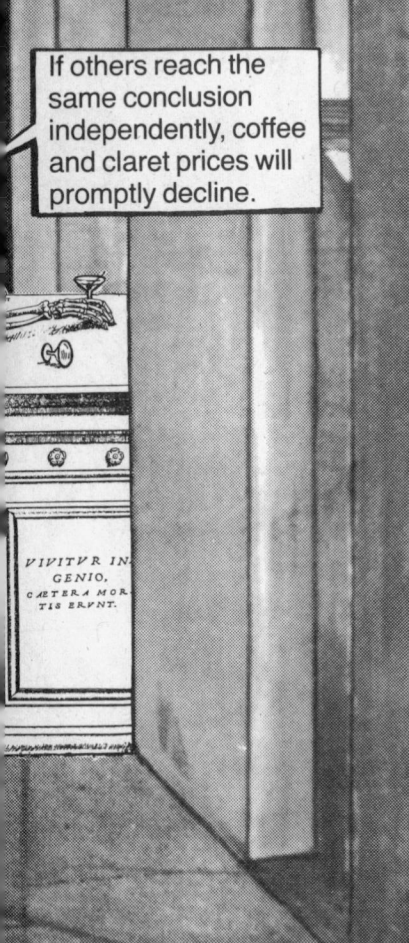

If others reach the same conclusion independently, coffee and claret prices will promptly decline.

VIVITVR IN
GENIO,
CÆTERA MOR
TIS ERVNT.

the market adjust their expectations according to the new information which incessantly flows in.

In the ideal free market economy, there are no labour unions. Nor are there giant corporations. Not only does no business firm dominate its industry, each enterprise is so small that no one notices when it folds. Collusion to rig prices or share markets is impossible because the numbers involved are too large to allow of successful conspiracy. There is little or no advertising. Competition is strictly over price and quality.

Government holds the ring and ensures fair play. A well-behaved set of politicians who understand their humble role defend the realm, administer criminal justice, and settle commercial disputes in the courts. For the rest, all that the public sector might reasonably add is construction of the few roads, harbours and lighthouses which are essential to trade and transportation but unattractive to private developers. In the handling of public budgets, national leaders aim at annually balanced accounts, the lowest possible level of taxes and the utmost frugality in their expenditure.

Myriads of men and women jostle each other for the jobs made available by numerous employers.
Aspiring employees seek alertly the best available combinations of wages, benefits, working conditions and promotion prospects.

Men and women are as free to test themselves in producer as in consumer roles. Capitalists are a self-nominated group. To join them is a matter of seizing an opportunity, mobilizing one's savings, borrowing from relatives, friends and banks, working hard and intelligently, and testing one's acumen and luck. If fortune smiles, you too may become as rich as Colonel Sanders of Kentucky Fried Chicken fame.

Take fair warning. Freedom to enrich oneself marches in step with freedom to go broke. The same caveat applies to capitalist freedom to choose vocations. Feel free to study art history, medieval Latin or classical Greek. Just don't be astounded or resentful that your agemates who cannily opted for business administration, econometrics and computer science drive better cars, live in bigger houses, and mix their drinks with better brands of liquor — for the next forty years.

Their prospective employers just as strenuously look for the best qualified candidates.

The hard lessons of the free market include individual responsibility for both success and failure.

27

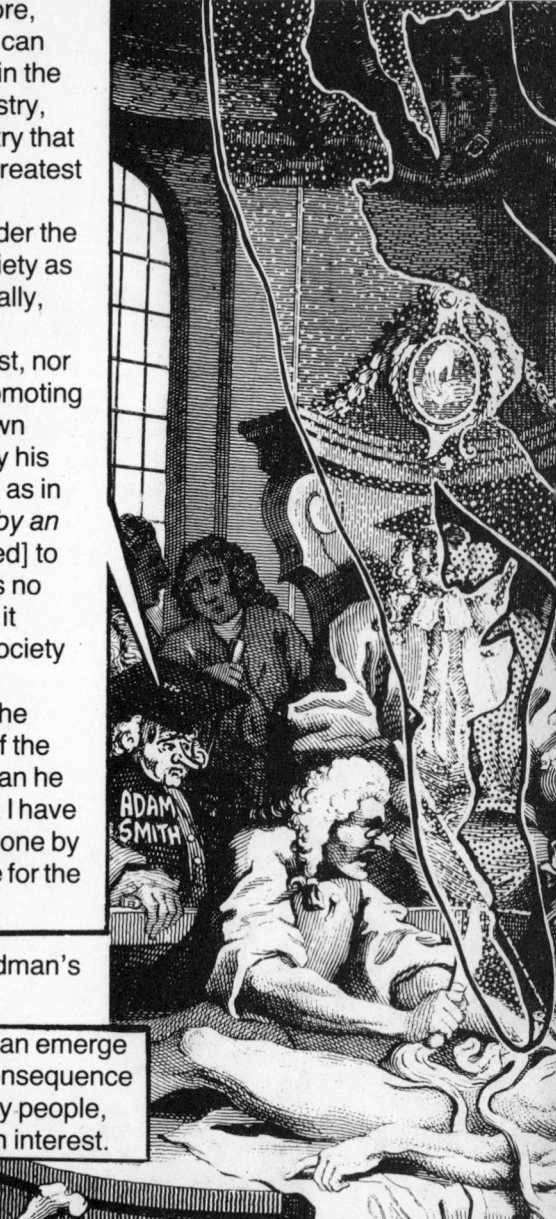

As every individual,therefore, endeavors as much as he can both to employ his capital in the support of domestick industry, and so to direct that industry that its produce may be of the greatest value, every individual necessarily labours to render the annual revenue of the society as great as he can. He generally, indeed, neither intends to promote the publick interest, nor knows how much he is promoting it . . . he intends only his own security . . . he intends only his own gain, and he is in this, as in many other cases, *led on by an invisible hand* [Italics added] to promote an end which was no part of his intention. Nor is it always the worse for the society that it was no part of it. By pursuing his own interest, he frequently promotes that of the society more effectually than he really intends to promote it. I have never known much good done by those who affected to trade for the publick good.

And remember Milton Friedman's point . . .

. . .economic order can emerge as the unintended consequence of the actions of many people, each seeking his own interest.

ADAM SMITH

Smith's abstract economic model, still supported by the monetarists today, is presented as if it were based on natural, indeed existential, human behaviour. Something crucial has been left out. And this is the first criticism of the free enterprise model.

❖❖❖❖❖❖❖❖❖❖❖❖❖❖❖❖❖❖❖

Origins Of The Market

Where does the "free market" come from? It wasn't created by God on the Eighth Day. Economists like Smith invent their market models by abstracting their features from the history and the actual institutional arrangements of the capitalist economies.

Markets do not spring from the pages of treatises. They evolve from human relationships, technological change, and legal systems. Buying and selling under the aegis of corporations and small entrepreneurs are comparatively recent phenomena. Even in the early days of capitalism, workers were less than free to move from place to place and barter their skill and strength for the best wages. Nor were their employers during the era of mercantilism or commercial capitalism in the 16th, 17th, and 18th centuries legally entitled to fabricate and sell what they pleased at any price they could coax customers to pay.

BRIEF HISTORY OF CAPITALISM
1. Mercantilism

Marx and later economic historians agree that modern, industrial capitalism began in 18th century Britain within the context of mercantilist ideology. Capitalists were not the heroes of mercantilism. Its central figure was the authoritarian monarch. The mercantilist state aimed at the enlargement of national power, not the gratification of individual aspirations to material advancement. Only the monarch truly embodied the realm's general interest; and only he could guide and manipulate economic affairs.

Mercantilist sovereigns engaged in high stakes, zero-sum games. In a poker game or any other zero-sum contest, the losses of some players just match the winnings of the others. In the game of nations, England could prosper only at France's or Spain's expense and vice versa. All contenders kept score by counting the gold and silver which travelled in and out of royal exchequers.

Mercantile capitalism became a genuine zero-sum game only after gold and silver from the New World mines ran out. Until then, Europe had exploited the natives of Peru and Mexico.

For other countries, without mines, the only way to collect gold and silver was to run a favourable balance of trade: somehow arrange to sell the foreigners more of your goods and services than you buy from them. Collect the difference in specie — i.e. gold or silver.

The emphasis on precious metal made good sense. With gold and silver, a ruler could hire mercenaries, feed and arm them, and fight successful wars. Mercantilism featured a siege mentality in a garrison state. Life was supposed to be grim for most citizens. Ordinary workers, the "poor" in revealing 18th century parlance, were distrusted by their betters as innately lazy, frivolous and turbulent. The best way to tame them was set them at work very young on very low wages.

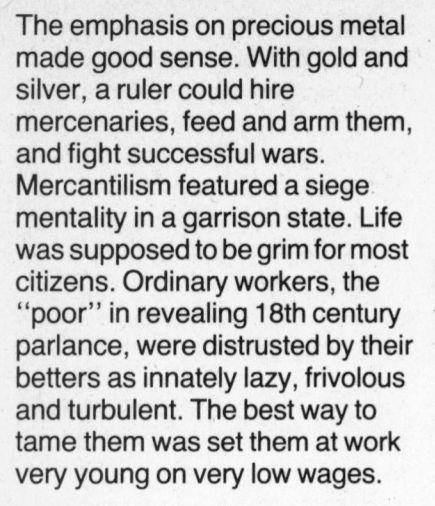

OH YES. AFTER THIS 14-HOUR NIGHT SHIFT I'M A PROFLIGATE LITTLE TEARAWAY...

Given the lower level of technology in mercantilist days, the way to extract maximum profits from labour was by extending the working day and the working life into childhood, and by keeping wages down below subsistence level. There were plenty of workers to keep the reserves of labour high.

For mercantilists low wages were appropriate for two reasons. The lower the average wage the more successfully English merchandise competed in foreign markets, enlarged the favourable balance of trade, and quickened the flow of specie into royal coffers. In addition, meager wages deprived their recipients of any temptation to buy foreign luxuries like tea, sugar, and cotton cloth.

Mercantilists did their considerable best to discourage mass consumption.

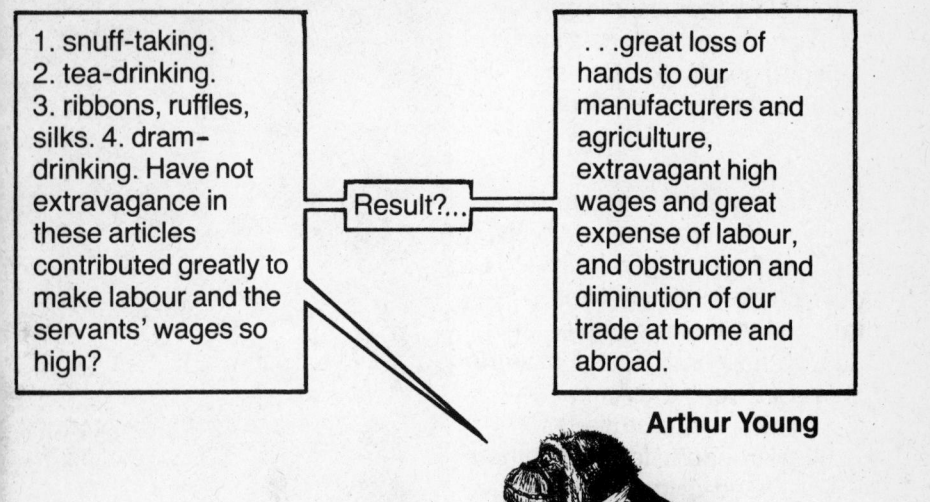

1. snuff-taking.
2. tea-drinking.
3. ribbons, ruffles, silks. 4. dram–drinking. Have not extravagance in these articles contributed greatly to make labour and the servants' wages so high?

Result?...

. . .great loss of hands to our manufacturers and agriculture, extravagant high wages and great expense of labour, and obstruction and diminution of our trade at home and abroad.

Arthur Young

Mercantilist regulations extended to importers, who were under steady suspicion of illegally sending specie out of the country.

It was a charge from which they could clear themselves only by converting raw materials into finished goods exported at substantially higher prices.

Colonies were required to ship timber, iron, tobacco, and beaver skins to Britain and refrain dutifully from competitive fabrication of ships, implements, cutlery, hats and shoes. For some Sons of Liberty the American Revolution was a crusade for political freedom; for many others it was a God-given chance to make more money.

> Real capitalism had to free itself from mercantilist regulations.

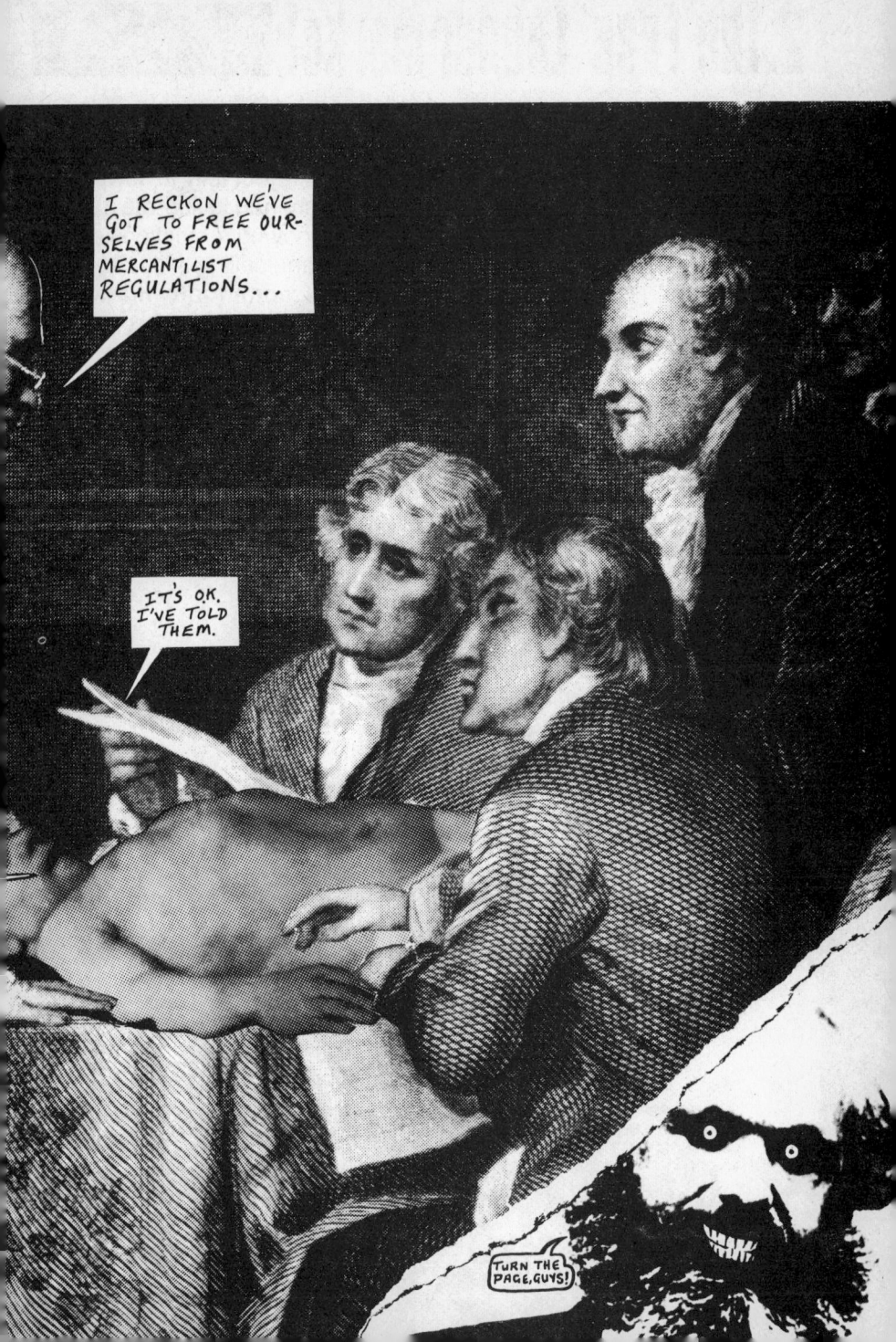

2. The `Free´ Labour Market

As Marx pungently demonstrated, fully to flower capitalism had to liberate itself from annoying restrictions on buying and selling in its two major markets: **commodity markets** in which all parties could compete without government interference and **labour markets** in which the energies of workers, their labour power, could be routinely bought and sold just like raw materials, finished goods, grain or any other commodity.

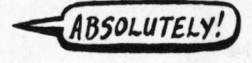

ABSOLUTELY!

THE INDUSTRIAL REVOLUTION

In that second market, the hunt for "free" labour, was located capitalism's greatest organizational challenge. How could the cotton mill magnates of the Industrial Revolution in 18th century Britain induce any rational human being to imprison himself in one of the grim new factories which James Watt's steam engine and parallel innovations in spinning and weaving rendered technically and organizationally feasible?
In these penitentiaries of body and spirit, working conditions were horrible, hours almost unendurably long, and payment wretched. Only adults confronted by starvation could endure such an environment, much less consign their young children to it.

When these children are four years old, they shall be sent to the county workhouse and there taught to read two hours a day and be kept fully employed the rest of their time in any of the manufactures of the house which best suits their age, strength and capacity. If it be established that at these early years they cannot be made useful, I reply that at four years of age there are sturdy employments in which children can earn their living; but, besides, there is considerable use in their being, somehow or other, constantly employed at least twelve hours in a day, whether they earn their living or not; for by these means we hope that the rising generation will be so habituated to constant employment that it would at length prove agreeable and entertaining to them. **JJ**

William Temple

It needed a catastrophe, the so-called Enclosure Movement, to provide an army of cheap labour for England's new factories.

Beginning in Elizabethan times, until the mid-19th century, proprietors enclosed open land with hedges or fences for sheep grazing. The reason for this was wool, England's most profitable export. The peasant, known as the yeoman in England, lost his traditional right to use the "common land" to graze his goat or cow and to till the land he needed to maintain his economic independence.

Peasants were destroyed as a class throughout Britain. A new economic individual was created — the landless worker, with nothing to sell but his or her **labour** for whatever the market offered.

The days of the self-sufficient yeomen were over. Enclosures drove them out of the countryside as paupers into the towns, cities and new factories.

As late as 1820, the Duchess of Sutherland dispossessed 15,000 tenants from 794,000 acres of land, replaced them with 131,000 sheep and rented her evicted families an average of 2 acres of submarginal land.

In Marx's mordant language, enclosure 'freed' workers from agricultural production and turned them into commodities, owners of saleable labour power. Here was the new industrial proletariat; not the skilled medieval artisan of once upon a time, protected by ancient rules and regulations.

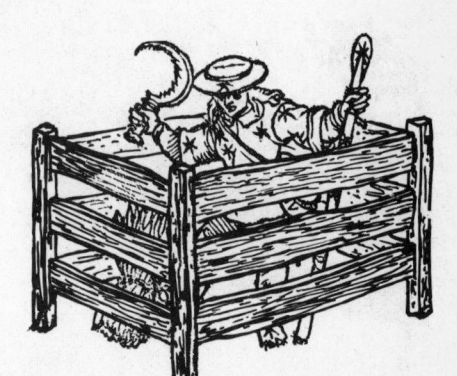

As for the situation of farmers who succeeded in clinging to the soil, two 20th century historians described it this way:
J.L. and Barbara Hammond

In the enclosed village at the end of the eighteenth century the position of the agricultural labourer was very different. All his auxiliary resources had been taken from him, and he was now just a wage earner and nothing more. Enclosure had robbed him of the strip that he tilled, of the cow that he kept on the village pasture, of the fuel that he picked up in the woods, and of the turf that he tore up from the common. And while a social revolution had swept away his possessions, an industrial revolution had swept away his family's earnings. To families living on the scale of the village poor, each of these losses was a crippling blow, and the total effect of the changes was to destroy their economic independence.

Enclosure, steam power, and the mechanization of the textile industry swept away the remnants of mercantilist regulation and prepared England by the end of the 18th century for a new era of unrestrained capitalism.

3. So That's »The Wealth Of Nations«...

The times needed a prophet to bless the emerging order. In 1776, Adam Smith's **The Wealth of Nations** became the sacred text for devotees of free markets, right up to the day of Milton Friedman and Margaret Thatcher.

But Smith was no apologist for the new class of industrial capitalists. His heroes were industrious artisans and energetic small businessmen. What counts, however, is less what a thinker says than the uses to which his theories are put. Much in **The Wealth of Nations** served the

convenience of the new capitalists. Smith did celebrate free trade at home and abroad. He did assert that the selfish and unrestrained pursuit of self-interest would improve the general welfare. He did prescribe a natural order in which the role of government was minimal.

These were the messages agreeable to industrialists because they were behaving in ways endorsed by Smith before **The Wealth of Nations** became popular. Still, it is always reassuring to be informed on good authority that private profit translates into public benefit.

WHOSE WEALTH?

The past is embodied in the present. In the 1980s England remains a society of large landowners who frequently trace their titles and properties back to 18th century enclosures. Much of London's prime real estate belongs to a handful of families. Ancient injustices make opulent the lives of living men and women, several generations removed from the events which enriched them.

The picture is remarkably similar throughout the western capitalist economies.

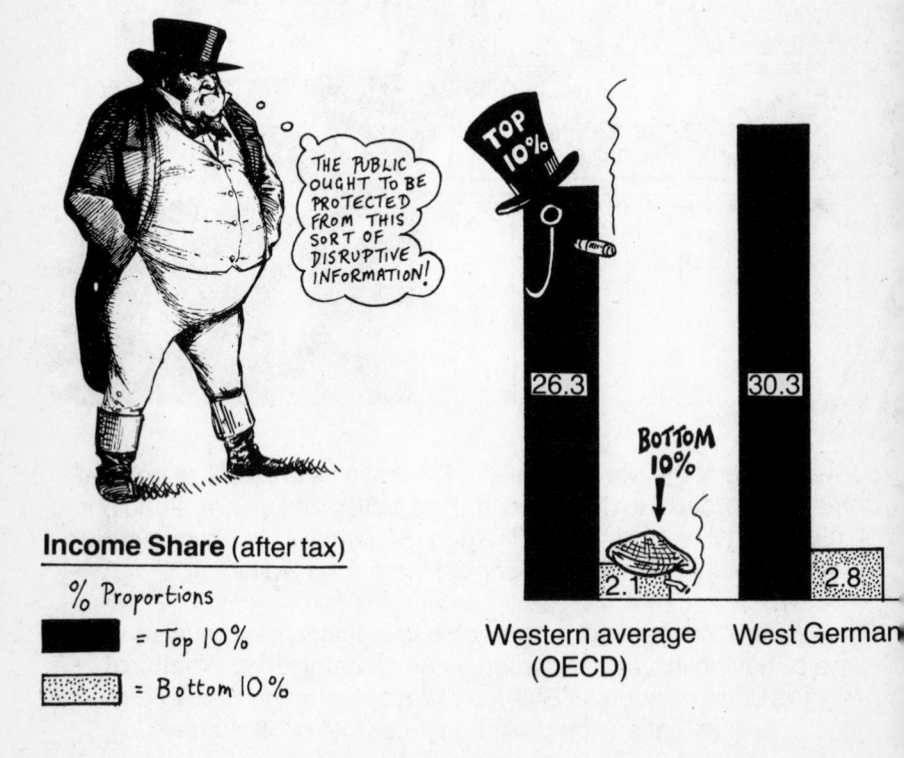

THE PUBLIC OUGHT TO BE PROTECTED FROM THIS SORT OF DISRUPTIVE INFORMATION!

TOP 10%

26.3

30.3

BOTTOM 10%

2.1

2.8

Income Share (after tax)

% Proportions

= Top 10%

= Bottom 10%

Western average (OECD)   West German

In the UK the top 10% of the population owns four-fifths of all personal wealth. The top 1% owns no less than 80% of all privately held company stocks and shares, with the top 10% owning 98% of them. The bottom 80% of the population owns just 10% of the personal wealth, mostly in the form of owning the house they live in. In other words, a tiny proportion of the population wields almost all the economic power.

[In West Germany, 1.7% of private households owns 75% of all stocks, shares and enterprises, and 31% of all personal wealth.]

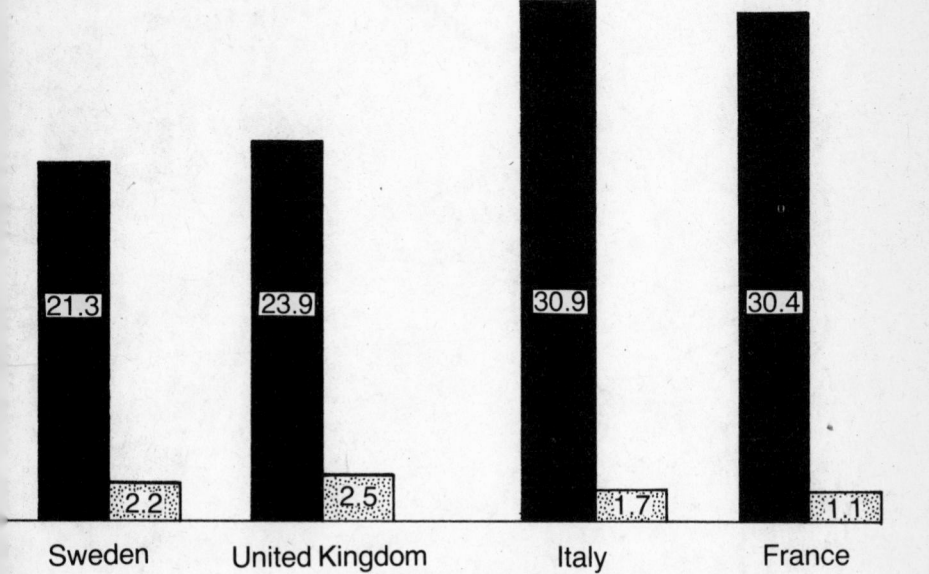

Sweden	United Kingdom	Italy	France
21.3	23.9	30.9	30.4
2.2	2.5	1.7	1.1

IS THE FREE MARKET JUST A MYTH?

Finding the ideally competitive market in reality is like hunting for that mythical creature, the unicorn. It was believed that only a "virgin without blemish" could capture the unicorn. No one pretends that capitalism is perfect, an unblemished virgin.

But the point is, do capitalism's real imperfections make it impossible for the market to exist, or operate, as freely as it's supposed to, according to capitalist theory?

Let's see what these imperfections are – and whether they refute capitalism's own claims about the freedoms of the market.

1. Obstacles To Market Freedom

Adam Smith himself was critical of early capitalism. His estimate of capitalists was as sceptical as his sympathy for their employees was generous.

Our merchants and master manufacturers complain much of the bad effects of high wages in raising the price, and thereby lessening the sale of their goods at home and abroad. They say nothing concerning the bad effects of their own gains. They complain only of those of other people.

People of the same trade rarely meet together, even for merriment and diversion, but the conversation ends in a conspiracy against the public, or in some contrivance to raise prices.

Smith's fears were justified. Tamperings with the market mechanism abound.

Monopoly exists whenever a single seller controls an entire market. **Shared monopolies** or **cartels** occur when a small number of sellers carve up the market to their own mutual satisfaction.

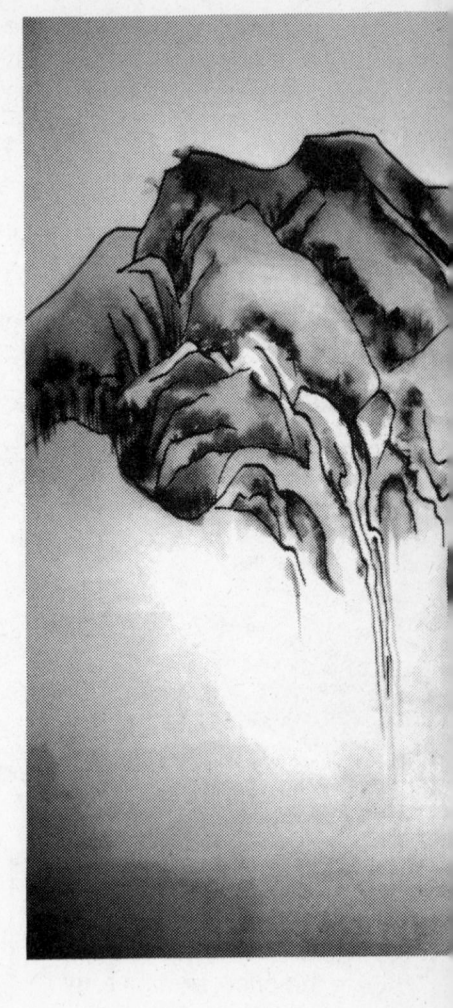

Oligopoly, common in countries like the United States which have made cartels illegal, prevails when a small number of large sellers informally arrange to refrain from price competition and focus their rivalry on advertising and minor differences in styling and packaging.

In all the important capitalist countries, free markets even approximating economists' ideas are limited to a portion of retailing, the stock exchanges, and a shrinking number of small manufacturing specialties.

2. Corporations

In Britain, Unilever is an example of corporate monopoly, as are the bread manufacturers and others who practise market concentration.

In Japan, powerful trading groups like Mitsubishi and Mitsui, in association with major banks and the central government, dominate important markets. In France, the **commissariat du plan**, in league with huge corporations and banks, channels investment, tax benefits, and outright public subsidies to preferred sectors of the economy.

In Europe, the EEC is based on price-level protectionism. For instance, the Multifibre Agreement limits imports of textiles into the EEC from the Third World.

In Britain, the anti-monopoly weapon is the Monopolies Commission, and the Prices and Incomes Board, now defunct. The United States, with its capitalist dedication to competition, has nearly a century-long history of statutory prohibition of monopoly. But the facts tell a different story. In 78 separate industries, among them autos, photographic equipment, tires, and aircraft, four huge corporations control at least 60 percent of their industry's sales.

Big corporations tend to get still bigger. In 1947, the largest 50 manufacturers controlled 17 percent of the entire manufacturing market. By 1972 the figure was 25 percent. Within the same time span the top 100 rose from 23 to 33 percent and the leading 200 from 30 to 43 percent. This is the privately planned sector of the economy which does most of American industry's research and development, markets a steady flow of new products, and shapes the market for them with a relentless barrage of print and television advertising. These are the firms which hate price competition. They raise prices in good times and bad, almost always preferring smaller sales at higher per unit profit to larger volume at lower per unit margins. That's the way Galbraith's planned sector of the economy operates.

John Kenneth Galbraith

The two parts of the economy —
the world of the few hundred
technically dynamic, massively
capitalized and highly organized
corporations on the one hand and
of the thousands of small and
traditional proprietors on the other
— are very different. It is not a
difference of degree but a
difference which invades every
aspect of economic organization
and behavior, including the
motivation to effort itself. It will be
convenient . . . to have a name for
the part of the economy which is
characterized by the large
corporations . . . I shall refer to it
as the Industrial System. The
Industrial System . . . is the
dominant feature of the New
Industrial State.

3. Multinationals

World capitalism is dominated by multinational companies who obey neither laws imposed by national governments nor the supposed 'free' market mechanisms so cherished by today's monetarists. Of the largest economic powers in the world, 57 are countries – but **43** are multinational companies!

General Motors (US) and Exxon (US) are larger than Yugoslavia, Switzerland or Saudi Arabia. BP (UK) wields more economic clout than Bulgaria, Greece or Finland.

General Motors' sales exceed the Gross National Product of most of the members of the United Nations. ITT's revenues exceed those of Portugal.

Of the top 50 multinationals, 21 are based in the United States. They have 54% of the total sales, with West German companies commanding 10%, the UK 9%, the Japanese 7%, the French 6% and the Dutch 5%.

53

No less than one-third of all world trade now consists of multinational companies trading with themselves. The UN recently estimated that some 50% of all US exports were within multinational companies themselves, and 30% of UK exports. But where the same organization is both buyer and seller, the market mechanism does not apply. The corporation can charge itself what it likes for its own products.

I'LL SWAP YOU THIS BAG OF MONEY FOR YOUR COLLECTION OF ARMAMENTS FACTORIES

THROW IN A PAI OF NUCLEAR REACTORS AND YOU'RE ON!

This massive opportunity to fix prices allows multinationals to:

*shift profits to where taxes are lowest, by over-invoicing imports to, or under-invoicing exports from, high tax countries.

*make 'loss making' sections of the firm break even by billing profitable foreign subsidiaries.

*strengthen their bargaining hand with trade unions by fixing profits downwards (e.g. Ford UK).

*where companies sell on a 'cost plus fixed profit' basis to governments, inflate their costs (drug companies selling to public health authorities).

*make profits from currency fluctuations.

*avoid exchange controls, circumvent tariffs and ease repatriation of profits.

Multinationals therefore make nonsense of the idea that there is a free market.

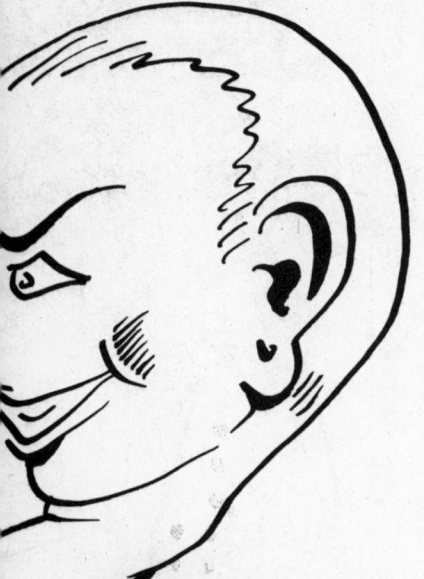

THE IMPACT OF MULTINATIONALS

The growth of these global giants owes much to post-war technological advance. Faster, cheaper forms of transport, computerized data systems and telecommunications networks combine to allow people and goods rapid movement, and tight control from the top of the corporation right around the globe.

"For business purposes," says the president of the IBM World Trade Corporation, "the boundaries that separate one nation from another are no more real than the equator. They are merely convenient demarcations of ethnic, linguistic, and cultural entities. They do not define business requirements or consumer trends. Once management understands and accepts this world economy, its view of the marketplace – and its planning – necessarily expands. The world outside the home country is no longer viewed as a series of disconnected customers and prospects for its products, but as an extension of a single market."

The multinationals have been a driving force in the internationalization of production. Modern techniques, production and trade are no longer defined in terms of countries, but fragmented into a number of partial operations scattered across a global interlinked system. Multinationals in their

routine operations evince distinct preferences for the poorer, developing countries of the Third World not only because labour is cheap but because the politicians frequently are weaker and more susceptible to pressure and manipulation.

The world market factory of the multinational is probably sited in a Free Trade Zone in a Third World country. Here it enjoys the "five freedoms" from corporate income tax, import duties, property taxes and excise taxes, as well as all the monetary and political incentives, such as no unions, granted by Third World states desperate for foreign capital and technology.

The new processing technologies combine automated capital-intensive production of some components in the developed countries with unskilled or semi-skilled assembly of the components, at various stages, in the developing countries. Cheap and well disciplined labour has become an important commodity in a world of increasingly sophisticated, technological capital-intensive industries. For example, the high technology silicon chips on which the electronics revolution is based

are assembled manually, under a microscope, by semi-skilled young women in the Free Trade Zones of South East Asia.

For the most advanced countries this means nationally based industries that have a vital multinational component. The future of Lockheed is linked to the future of US capitalism, but also, to a lesser extent, to that of Rolls Royce. The future of Ford depends both on the US market, and on Ford Europe. IBM's activities, although skewed in favour of the home base, form an integrated international operation.

What is true of American capitalism, which has the largest national base, is even more true of smaller capitalist countries like Britain. Here some of the leading industries have reached the point where their overseas investments are in the same league as their domestic investments. As E.D. de Windt, of the Eaton Corporation, put it: "The World Company, owned, managed, and operated without regard to the physical, political, and philosophical boundaries of nationalism can well become a reality . . . " Or in the words of Jacques Maisonrouge, ex-chairman of IBM: "They (multinationals) are building what, for all intents and purposes must be considered a new world economic system: one in which the constraints of geography have yielded to the

logic of efficiency." Fiat's Aurelio Peccei commented that the global corporation " is the most powerful agent for the internationalization of human society."

THE MULTINATIONALS: AGENTS OF IMPERIALISM

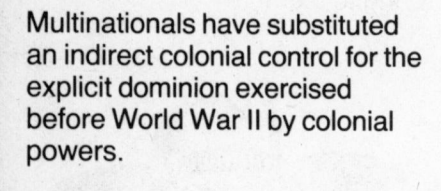

Multinationals have substituted an indirect colonial control for the explicit dominion exercised before World War II by colonial powers.

1.   Multinationals have distorted production patterns by substituting in Brazil and elsewhere the cash crops of commercial agriculture for achievable self-sufficiency in food and fiber.

2.   They have frequently edged out small indigenous entrepreneurs.

3.   Giant food conglomerates have harmfully altered consumption choices by marketing soft drinks, junk foods, and similar low priority items in poor societies. Even worse, they have heavily promoted cigarettes and marketed drugs elsewhere prohibited as unsafe or inefficacious. The Swiss-based giant Nestlé gained notoriety by pushing infant feeding formulas which threatened the health of Third World infants.

4. The ethics of the global conglomerates are those of the marketplace: give as little as possible and take as much as is politically acceptable.

Investigations by the US Senate revealed that by 1977, 360 US companies admitted to giving bribes in foreign countries. The 95 largest had paid out $1 billion each over the past few years. In Britain, the major scandal was that of the oil companies, who continued to supply the illegal Rhodesian regime with oil for over ten years, despite government sanctions.

5. ITT is famous for the role it played in overthrowing the popularly elected Chilean administration of Salvador Allende. The Arabian-American Oil Company (ARAMCO), the Anglo-Dutch-American consortium of energy goliaths which operates Saudi Arabian oil fields, briefly denied oil to the American Sixth Fleet stationed in the Mediterranean during the 1973 Yom Kippur war. On that occasion, ARAMCO's foreign policy was that of OPEC.

6. Often, multinationals actually export more capital from developing countries than they bring to them.

7.   Often a consequence of intense multinational activity is creation of a small modern sector amid actual intensification of the poverty of the traditional economy, much as occurred in the Shah's Iran.

8.   The profits of alert multi-nationals have much less to do with their efficiency and sensitivity to customer preferences than with their astuteness in lobbying, bribery, and mutually profitable alliances with the politicians of many countries. Everywhere they appear to operate as a mongrel blend of politics and economics, negotiating tax concessions, subsidies, protections against unions, sheltered markets, and allied benefits from local, regional, and national governments. In the western capitalist societies, the weaker multinationals have demonstrated considerable talent for enlisting government in time of need, as Britain bailed out British Leyland and Rolls-Royce, and the Carter administration rescued Chrysler. Already in 1980, one major US bank, First Philadelphia, and one major financier have had to be rescued by the administration. The Chrysler bail money has been upped; and while two million UK jobs depend on British Leyland's fortunes, it will not be allowed to go to the wall.

4. Externalities: Cost-Shifting & Pollution

All kinds of markets, competitive or otherwise, share another grave defect, which even conventional economics has come to recognize as important. "Externalities" define the capacity of producers to evade some of their costs by shifting

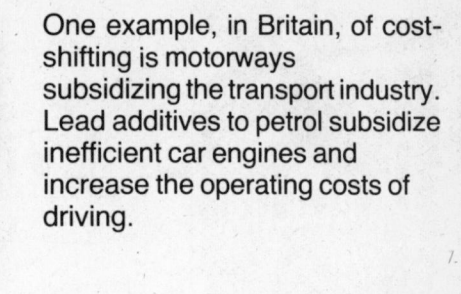

One example, in Britain, of cost-shifting is motorways subsidizing the transport industry. Lead additives to petrol subsidize inefficient car engines and increase the operating costs of driving.

Pollution is the grave social consequence of cost-shifting. Rio Tinto Zinc's Avonmouth smelter, in Britain, pours out pollution. Pulp and paper mills dump noxious chemicals into streams and foul odors into the air. Until recently at least, long stretches of Rhine and Rühr riverbeds functioned as disposal sites for waste chemicals.

them either to customers or to the public at large.

Until the Japanese government imposed anti-pollution restraints, Tokyo pedestrians were compelled to don nose masks to filter out the grosser pollutants in the air. Only against intense corporate opposition, the American Environmental Protection Agency has compelled installation of anti-pollution equipment in electrical generating plants, steel mills, chemical facilities, and other major generators of pollution.

It is hard to see how unrestrained self-interest can ever add up to the public good. But, according to Smith's theory, a businessman is not a moral monster if he shifts on to his employees the medical burdens of industrial accidents and carcinogenic substances.

It costs money and diminishes potential profit to instal safety equipment and monitor the use of dangerous materials. In the rush for quick profit, a "reputable" pharmaceutical firm marketed thalidomide, an inadequately tested drug prescribed for pregnant women. The distressing consequence was the birth of dozens of sadly deformed infants, some without arms or legs, in England and western Europe. In the United States, Hooker Chemical, a subsidiary of Occidental Petroleum, a major oil company, dumped so many noxious chemicals in upper New York State's Love Canal that a severe public health program ensued.

5. Inequalities Of Opportunity

If the market were really free, perfectly competitive, shouldn't everyone enter it on equal terms? Capitalists argue that you can get what you want from it, even if you start out poor and disadvantaged.

Look at Abe Lincoln — he started from a log cabin. And I started above a grocery shop!

We've seen how wealth is unequally distributed. The same is true of incomes. Examples. The average industrial wage in Britain is about £90 per week. Compare this with Arnold Weinstock, head of GEC, whose income in 1979 was about £1½ million.

The American distribution in 1977 revealed that the lowest fifth of households collected 5.6% of total income and the highest fifth 38.1%. By 1979, the minimum wage in the United States had risen to $2.90 per hour and the head of General Motors earned over $1 million in salary and bonuses.

AND I EARN EVERY BRASS NICKEL OF IT

And it's more or less the same story in all the developed countries.

There are two ways of looking at the inequality of economic reward. The capitalist says that unequal income is essential to an efficient economy. Self-interest is an important impetus to effort, saving and investment. Besides, some people are brighter, more imaginative or energetic than others, so it's only fair that their rewards should be higher. A socialist would argue that inequality reflects the power relationships of capitalism.

Either way, inequality under capitalism is taken as **necessary** and inevitable.

Inherited wealth also distorts the "ideal" operation of competitive markets.

IF I LEAVE YOUNG HENRY ALL MY MONEY WILL IT GO TO HIS HEAD?...

1. Great fortunes acquired a century or longer ago endow their contemporary beneficiaries with influence over the direction of investment which has not been earned by any contribution of their own.

2. Inheritance favours heirs with extra benefits of many kinds. As children, they are enrolled in the best schools, offered chances to travel, given the self-confidence of social acquaintance with the cultured and powerful, and, as an effect of these experiences, improved chances of admission to elite colleges and professional schools. When the children of the affluent enter professional job markets, doors swing open to them in their parents' enterprises or those of friends of the family.

3. Inheritance skews the political process. The wealthy wield the resources to finance their own campaigns for office or those of friendly politicians. By the same token, they can finance opponents of unfriendly office holders. Like the commercial marketplace the political arena is fueled by cash.

Then, again, what about inherited race and sex?

One can no more choose one's skin pigmentation than the size of the family fortune.

In the United States, black college graduates earn two-thirds or less of the amounts collected by similarly educated white males. At the end of 1979, unemployment among all teenagers was 16.09 percent. For black teenagers it was more than twice as high.

Nor can the child choose his or her sex. In all the advanced capitalist economies, women earn substantially less than men when the two sexes are carefully matched by education and other marketable qualifications. As upon blacks and other minorities, the burden of unemployment falls heavily upon them. Again at the end of 1979, unemployment among male heads of families was 2.8 percent, for women in the same status 8.4 percent.

In sum, much of the inequality under capitalism is not required as an incentive to effort and investment. It amounts, therefore, to unjust enrichment of a few at the expense of a great many others.

Instability, Crisis ß Business Cycles

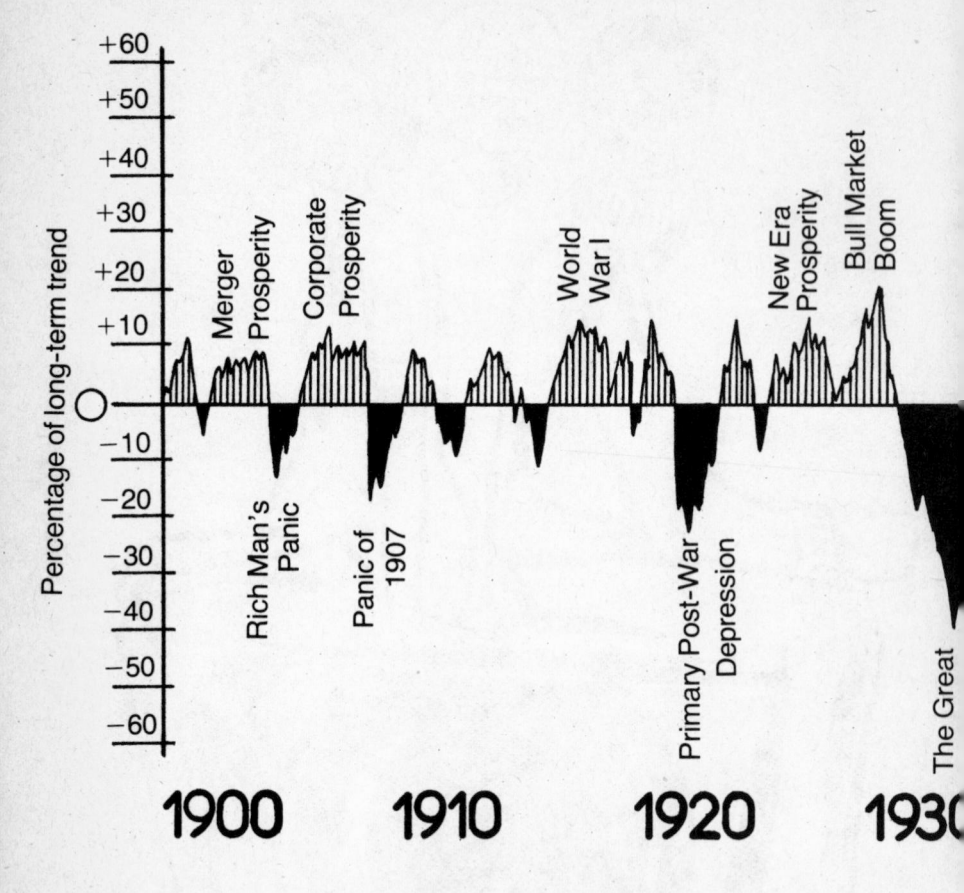

Percentage of long-term trend

+60 +50 +40 +30 +20 +10 0 −10 −20 −30 −40 −50 −60

Merger Prosperity

Corporate Prosperity

World War I

New Era Prosperity

Bull Market Boom

Rich Man's Panic

Panic of 1907

Primary Post-War Depression

The Great

1900　1910　1920　1930

All through its history, capitalism has also been marred by repetitive instability – the business cycle.

In the United States alone, since 1855 there have been twenty-five business cycles, some short and comparatively painless; others, like the Great Depression of the 1930s, disasters which idled more than a quarter of the working population, closed numerous factories, bankrupted large numbers of farmers and business enterprises, and cost the economy countless billions of dollars of lost output of goods and services.

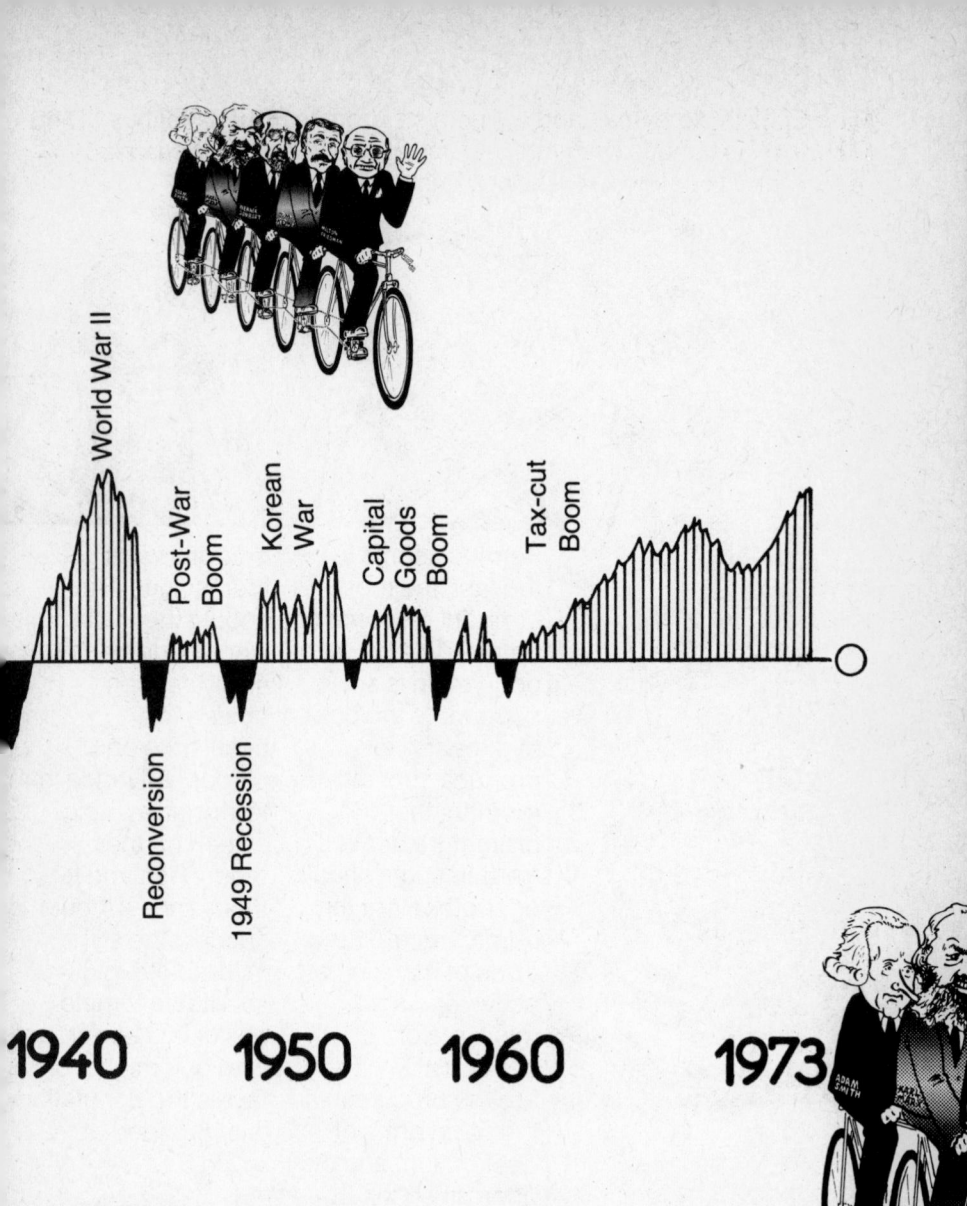

World War II

Post-War Boom

Korean War

Capital Goods Boom

Tax-cut Boom

Reconversion

1949 Recession

1940   1950   1960   1973

The business cycle is the child of the Industrial Revolution and the emergence of modern capitalism. This is no claim that daily life for average residents of 17th and 18th century Europe was idyllic. Most families survived on the thin edge of destitution. A failed harvest, a damaging war, a natural disaster imposed actual hunger. But these were taken to be acts of God or wilful sovereigns, not regular economic occurrences.

73

The English clergyman and economist Thomas Robert Malthus (1766-1835) in his famous essay on population (1798) aptly summarized economic life before the advent of the business cycle.

Famine seems to be the last, the most dreadful resource of nature. The power of population is so superior to the power of the earth to produce substance for man, that premature death must in some shape or another visit the human race. The vices of mankind are active and able ministers of depopulation. They are the precursors in the great army of destruction; and they often finish the dreadful work themselves. But should they fail in this war of extermination, sickly season, epidemics, pestilence and plague, advance in terrific array, and sweep off their thousands and ten thousands. Should success be still incomplete, gigantic, inevitable famine stalks in the rear, and with one mighty blow, levels the population with the food of the world.

This was the passage that induced Thomas Carlyle, himself not the most cheerful of prophets, to dub political economy the dismal science.

DISMAL

Malthus' point was distinct: the business cycle was not yet among the calamities which afflicted the human race.

YOU DON'T LIKE IT? —GO TO RUSSIA!!

T.C.

Marx's Explanation OVERPRODUCTION

Students of the business cycle still disagree about its causes and cures, without substantially improving on the clues which Marx furnished in the last century. One was the persistent tendency of capitalism to produce too much, from the standpoint of sellers unable to rid themselves at profitable prices of their merchandise. It was not that workers didn't want the stuff, but that they lacked the income to buy it.

The enormous power, inherent in the factory system, of expanding by jumps, and the dependence of that system on the markets of the world, necessarily begets feverish production, followed by overfilling of the markets, whereupon contraction of the markets brings on crippling of production.

FALLING RATE OF PROFIT

A still more crucial clue was the tendency of profit to fall. Marx believed that the single source of profit was the surplus value extracted by capitalists from their employees, the difference between the price of labour power [wages] and the sales receipts derived from the disposal of the products of that labour power. Capitalism, as a technologically progressive social form, tends persistently to substitute machines for human workers. Hence labour power, the source of surplus value, tends to contract and with it the rate of profit.

Marx carefully stated this law as a tendency which, in the short run or a series of short runs, could be checked in several ways.

1. Temporarily the rate of exploitation might be increased. If the average worker laboured harder and devoted a smaller proportion of each day to his own support, a larger fraction of his output would add to his employer's profit.

A multinational corporation, using the same equipment, will make more money in Hong Kong or Taiwan than in Amsterdam or Munich, because it will pay much lower wages. The Asian worker works fewer hours for himself and more hours for his employer than does his European or American counterpart.

2. Marx assumed that wages moved towards a subsistence level, regulated partly by the physiological needs of workers and their families and partly by conventional, social definitions of "minimum" at different periods and in different places. However, during recessions when unemployment is high, wages might temporarily be forced below subsistence, the rate of surplus value enlarged, and profits commensurately increased.

3. On some occasions, the price of machinery may be reduced as a result of technological innovation. For example, minicomputers costing a few hundred pounds (or dollars) can now do the work of a huge machine that used to cost tens of thousands. The cost of one unit of computer memory fell a thousand-fold between 1970 and 1979.

When machinery costs less, total invested capital increases more slowly even as equipment replaces human labour.

4.——▶

77

4. A benefit to capitalists of foreign trade is its capability of cheapening the food and raw materials which enter into working class diet and clothing. Lower prices of necessities diminish the level of subsistence wages. Such precisely was the impact of the English Corn Laws in 1846. After that date, unimpeded import of cheap American grain substantially reduced the cost of living and the minimum price of labour.

Summing Up

Criticism of capitalism falls into two categories: a) capitalism's failures **in its own terms**, imperfect markets, failing investment and so on; and b) the inhumane **side-effects** of this system on those who have to live under it, unfair incomes, pollution, etc.

For the Marxists, criticism of imperfect price mechanisms or pollution does not go to the heart of understanding capitalism. For them, capitalism is based on a class system. A ruling class of property-owners exploits a proletariat of labourers, "freed" of any claim on property.

It is worth remembering that universal male suffrage was not gained in England till the late 1860s and 70s. Aneurin Bevan, the great British Labour leader, later commented on this:

"It is highly doubtful whether the achievements of the Industrial Revolution would have been permitted if the franchise had been universal. It is very doubtful because a great deal of the capital aggregations that we are at present enjoying are the results of the wages that our fathers went without.**"**

We've seen many of capitalism's wrongs. Can they be put right? Will the system fall?

1929: The Collapse Of Capitalism?

The Great Depression, 1929-39, convinced many that capitalism was staggering to its final crisis. England began its depression early in the 1920s. The German crisis brought Adolf Hitler to power. In the United States, where was out of work. Nine million savings accounts were lost as the banks collapsed. $30 billion in financial assets vanished when the stock market crashed. One in five of all Detroit schoolchildren was officially registered as undernourished by 1932.

There is still no completely convincing account of what caused the Great Depression. In the U.S. investment fell by 88% between 1929 and 1933. Other factors contributed to this collapse. Farm incomes had been falling for years. Profits were booming while wage income remained basically unchanged. Credit collapsed. Companies pyramided one atop the other fell like playing cards when the stock market fell. All this was worsened by a policy of tight money supply.

depression was deepest, GNP fell from $104 billion in 1929 to $56 billion in 1933. Unemployment soared from 1.5 million to 12.8 million, one person in four

Franklin Roosevelt's New Deal created some low paid public jobs and imparted a measure of general stimulus to the economy. But American unemployment in 1939, on the eve of World War II, hung at 14 percent and economists wrote gloomily of permanent stagnation. Closed frontiers, flagging technological innovation, and slowing population growth all threatened lasting unemployment and an end to the prospect of higher living standards.

An event and a theory rescued world capitalism and gave it a new lease on life. The event was World War II. In prenuclear times, a major war guaranteed full employment either in the armed services or in war industries. Moreover, the destruction inflicted by bombing guaranteed a reconstruction boom once the war ended.

DOLE QUEUE

The New Theory Of J.M. Keynes

The theory was the creation of John Maynard Keynes [1883 – 1946]. His 1936 classic, **The General Theory of Employment, Interest and Money**, transformed economic theory and public policy toward recession and depression.

Though a frequent critic of capitalism, Keynes was no socialist. Quite the contrary. Keynes's persistent object was to make capitalism perform more smoothly, equitably and humanely, especially in his native England.

How can I accept a doctrine which sets up as its Bible, above and beyond criticism, an obsolete economic textbook which I know to be not only scientifically erroneous but without interest or application to the modern world? How can I adopt a creed which, preferring the mud to the fish, exalts the boorish proletariat above the bourgeois and the intelligentsia, who, with whatever faults, are the quality in life and surely carry the seeds of all human advancement? Even if we need a religion, how can we find it in the rabid rubbish of the Red bookshops?

THIS LADY IS NOT AN ECONOMIST BUT LYDIA LOPOKOVA, THE FAMOUS BALLET DANCER (AND MRS. KEYNES)

Keynes On Macroeconomics

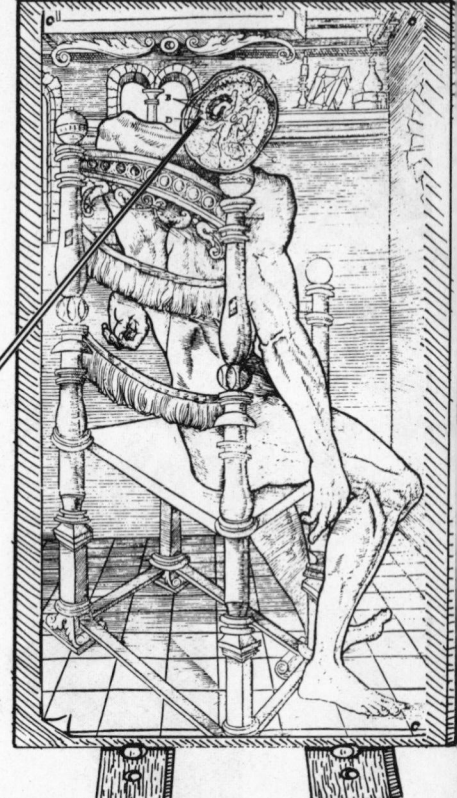

BUT **MICRO** WAS GOOD ENOUGH FOR ME...

Until Keynes the study of economics was almost entirely **microeconomics**, or price theory, analysis of individual prices in a sequence of markets. Price theorists sought to explain how sellers maximized their profits and buyers maximized the satisfactions or utilities that they sought from their purchases. The implicit and sometimes explicit assumption of price theory was that if markets were competitive,

business cycles were self-limiting. During recessions, sellers cut their prices and workers accepted lower wages. Soon recovery began without government intervention. The persistence of mass unemployment during the 1930s puzzled Keynes's colleagues, just as much as intractable inflation in the 1980s baffles their successors.

Keynes's explanation required invention of a new branch of economic theory. This was **macroeconomics**, which focused not on individual prices and markets but on aggregates like Gross National Product, national income, business investment, government expenditures, and, most important of all, the volume of employment.

The Theory Of Aggregate Demand

Why macroeconomics? To Keynes at least, it was glaringly evident that Adam Smith's invisible hand no longer worked. At the least it needed help. Keynes began with a fresh diagnosis of the disease of depression and mass unemployment. For him, it was above all an affliction caused by deficient **aggregate demand**, total dollar purchases by consumers, business investors and government. Keynes's central insight was simple and powerful: depression ensued whenever the combined expenditures of government and private parties were too small to furnish jobs for all the men and women who wanted them.

Why did spending lag? What induced consumers to spend more rather than less? What encouraged business to place orders for new buildings and machines today instead of next year or never? How do politicians make up their minds to raise or lower taxes, enlarge or contract public expenditures?

For all these queries, Keynes had ingenious answers. Start with consumers, who in rich societies do two-thirds or so of total spending. Consumers are a diverse lot upon whom many influences converge. Individual temperaments differ. Some men and women are spendthrifts, probably a smaller number are misers.
But one large generalization safely can be made. By and large, most people spend more as their incomes rise, and less when they fall.
Americans usually spend between 92 and 94 cents out of each dollar's added

income and save the remaining six or eight cents. In other words, consumers react to what happens to them.
Therefore, their behaviour cannot explain why aggregate demand moves either upward or downward.
It is the investing class who are the dynamic element.

89

2. INVESTORS

Businessmen enjoy much wider latitude of choice. When business is bad or a recession is feared,

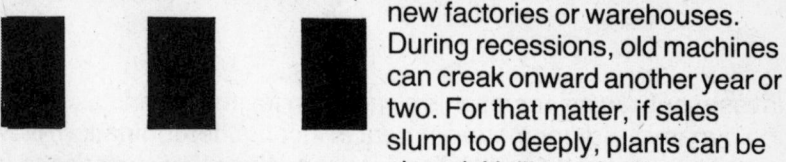

corporate managers can postpone purchases of new equipment and construction of new factories or warehouses. During recessions, old machines can creak onward another year or two. For that matter, if sales slump too deeply, plants can be closed. Unlike laid-off workers, company officials retain their jobs.

Consumers spend to survive. Investors can wait. Upon that contrast hangs the central point of Keynes's explanation of fluctuations in aggregate demand and employment. Precisely because investment is oriented to the future, it is extraordinarily volatile. To invest in a new factory or new equipment is to guess that hypothetical customers will agreeably appear and buy the proper quantities at the proper prices of shoes, ships, or sealing wax for the five, ten, or twenty years of the new investment's useful life.

No wonder that the animal spirits of businessmen, the waves of optimism and pessimism which wash over the investment community, seem to have more to do with violent swings of investment during business cycles than all the calculations of accountants, economists, and assorted wizards in corporate employ.

The Investment Multiplier

Investment always represents a wager on the future, and as such it is the dynamic, autonomous element in income determination. New investment sets off a **multiplier process**. When investors spend an extra $10 billion, they speedily place this sum in the pockets of workers, suppliers and contractors, and **national income**, the total payment to wage earners, stockholders, lenders and other income recipients, rises $10 billion.

This is only the beginning. The people who get the $10 billion spend most of it on consumer goods and services. Their behaviour in turn creates income for auto dealers, supermarket operators, department stores, airlines, and other sellers. If out of the initial $10 billion of new investment, consumers whose incomes have risen spend merely 90 percent, national income rises by an additional $9 billion in this second round of spending. There is an $8.1 billion third round, a $7.2 billion fourth round, and so on in an indefinite, diminishing progression.

National income eventually rises by $100 billion – the original $10 billion investment plus $90 billion of consumer spending sparked by the spending and respending of that $10 billion. The **investment multiplier**, the relation between an amount invested (here $10 billion) and the total impact on national income (here $100 billion), is 10.

This relatively simple mechanism has a fateful effect on public policy. Once the voters and their political representatives realize that investment is the key to prosperity and depression, government is expected to do something during bad times to revive investment.

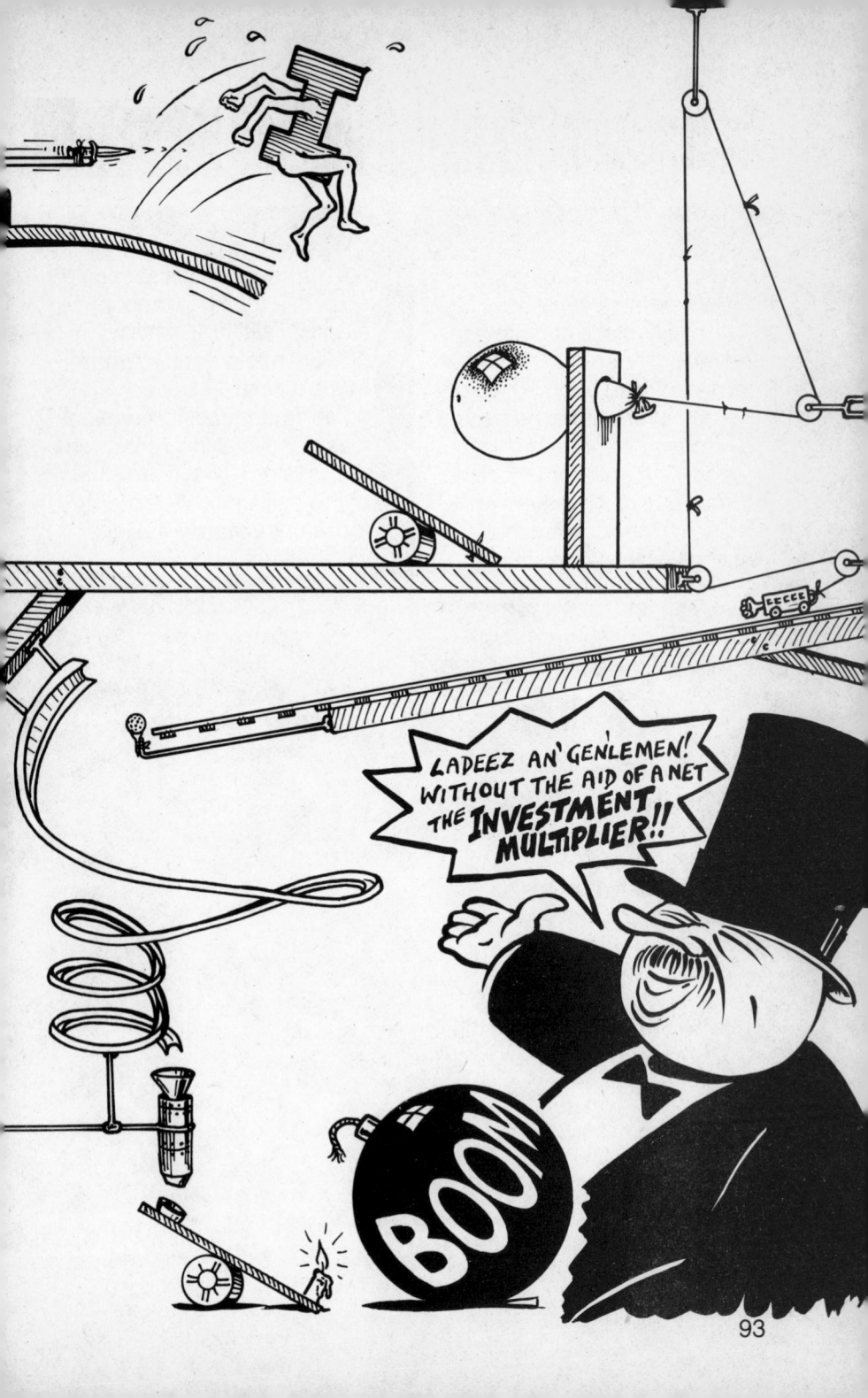

Government Deficit Spending

Keynes recommended that government must fill the investment slack and provide the missing demand. Common sense advised bringing together millions of unemployed people and massive unfilled social needs. Any government could readily pay new workers on its projects by borrowing the savings which were sitting uselessly in banks.

Government deficit spending sets off a multiplier sequence identical with that of new private investment. Keynes made it clear to any dolt that government deficit spending was beneficial in a recession or depression, even if the stupidity of the politicians dictated a foolish direction to the initial expenditure.

GOVERNMENT

"If the Treasury were to fill old bottles with banknotes, bury them at suitable depths in disused coal mines which are then filled up to the surface with town rubbish and then leave it to private enterprise on the well-tried principles of **laissez-faire** to dig the notes up again (the right to do so being obtained, of course, by tendering for leases of the note-bearing territory), there need be no more unemploymnent and, with the help of the repercussions, the real income of the community, and its capital wealth also, would probably become a good deal greater than it actually is. It would, indeed, be more sensible to build houses and the like; but if there are political and practical difficulties in the way of this the above would be better than nothing."

John Maynard Keynes

95

Keynes provided other extreme examples to show how useless effort might have useful consequences.

ER... YOU COULDN'T MAKE IT FOUR COULD YOU? THE WIFE'S NOT LOOKING TOO WELL.

Ancient Egypt was doubly fortunate, and doubtless owed its fabled wealth, in that it possessed **two** activities, namely pyramid building as well as the search for the precious metals, the fruits of which, since they could not serve the needs of man by being consumed, did not stale with abundance. Two pyramids, two masses for the dead are twice as good as one; but not two railways from London to York.

Keynes was no Marxist or even socialist. His theory, economic policy and recommendations for government intervention were consciously devised to combat the spectre of Marxism.

Keynes was gloomy about capitalist prospects. What he called the marginal efficiency of capital, and defined as the value today of the profits anticipated over the life of a machine or building, was likely to be so low that the outlook was a long-run deficit in investment, aggregate demand, and employment.

Keynes recommended a "somewhat comprehensive socialization of investment" and substantial redistribution of income in the direction of equality. Keynes dropped these explosive hints almost as afterthoughts to his theory of income determination. Of course, any society which nationalizes major industries and equitably redistributes income more nearly approaches socialism than capitalism.

Post-war capitalism seemed to take the shape Keynes had recommended, without turning socialist.
Let's see what happened after 1945.

The world system had never before grown so fast and for so long ☐

The Post-War 'Economic Miracle'

From a Keynesian standpoint, World War II constituted a large-scale demonstration that if enough money were available to spend for **any** purpose, full employment was the predictable consequence. Here was the latter-day equivalent of Egyptian pyramids and quests for precious metals. In the reconstruction decades after World War II, full employment, rapid economic growth, expanded welfare benefits, and reasonably stable prices all conspired to solidify capitalism's grip upon popular affection in the First World.

For twenty years after the Second World War, capitalism enjoyed a prolonged and quite unprecedented boom. The world system had never before grown so fast and for so long — twice as fast between 1950 and 1964 as between 1913 and 1950. Output rarely fell anywhere within the western capitalist countries, and at no point by more than two percentage points on an annual basis. Compare this with the preceding periods. Between the wars, output was below peak in most countries for one-third of the time, and there were falls of up to 20% in gross domestic product.

In France, Italy, and West Germany growth was rapid enough to place their residents in a situation of comparative affluence much greater than that of Britons who, at World War II's close, were much better off than either winners or losers in western Europe. The most sensational success story of all was Japan's tremendous surge of development which brought the country from the ruins of war devastation to number three ranking among the world's industrial economies.

The United States emerged from World War II with a powerful undamaged economy...

What Made The Post-War Boom Possible ■

1. Western Europe and Japan needed to rebuild war damaged economies. This urgency occasioned a surge in new factories, equipment, housing, schools, roads, and hospitals. Attracted by improved incomes, large numbers of farmers moved to cities and factory jobs, where their productivity was greater.

2. European and Japanese objectives and opportunities meshed smoothly with American interests. The United States emerged from World War II with a powerful, undamaged economy which dominated world markets. For several years, the United States was the single major source of exportable surpluses of food and manufactured goods.

3. Marshall Plan aid to western Europe and similar subsidies to Japan and West Germany supplied the dollars needed to buy grain and tobacco from American farms and finished goods from American factories.

The ideology of the cold war and the threat, real or otherwise, of Russian aggression rendered these subsidies acceptable to most Americans.

4. Under Keynesian inspiration but mostly American guidance, the Bretton Woods conference in 1944 established the **International Monetary Fund** [empowered to make short term loans to governments to prop up weak currencies] and the **World Bank** [equipped to lend funds for longer periods to developing nations].

5. Growth in the First World was facilitated by cheap energy and raw materials. Although England, France, and last of all Portugal accepted the independence of their colonial possessions, the neocolonialism which succeeded direct administration generally allowed western interests to retain control of resources in their former possessions.

. . . the Western European nations were too weak to participate in a free market.

The US emerged from the war as the world's wealthiest and most powerful capitalist nation. To consolidate this dominance, the American government hoped to create an interdependent, international economy based on multilateral free trade that would serve the interests of US capitalism in the way that free trade had fortified British capitalism in the 19th

The Quiet Americans?

century. But at the end of the war it was realized that the Western European nations were too weak to participate in a free market. Several had powerful pro-Moscow Communist Parties, and if their economies became any weaker, they were in danger of gravitating towards the Soviet Union. The Americans were confronted by a similar situation in the Far East where a defeated Japan lay close to the rising power of Chinese Communism.

US governments opted to build up buffer zones and assist their economic regeneration. They introduced the Marshall Aid Plan and encouraged the formation of the EEC — although a condition of American support for the Rome treaty was a guarantee that Common Market governments would treat American subsidiaries equally with their national firms. With its exports placed at a disadvantage in Europe's protected market, American industry intensified its export of manufacturing capacity.

The increasing spread of US affiliates abroad helped offset the financial burden of maintaining American military superiority, and maintained the US share of world markets by securing a strong position in foreign economies and controlling access to vital raw materials such as oil.

The 20 year boom was centred in the economy of the US. This created the conditions for the big increase in world trade which, in its turn, made possible the "economic miracle" in the heavily export-oriented economies of West Germany, Japan and elsewhere. It relied on the remarkable post-war technological revolution — the "second industrial revolution" as it is called.

The Europeans were forced to accept an international monetary system based around the special position of the US dollar. Through this system, established at the 1944 Bretton Woods conference, all currencies stood at fixed exchange rates to the US dollar, which was itself fixed at 35 dollars to the ounce of gold. While all other nations had to settle balance of payments deficits in gold, outstanding dollars were to be held in the reserves of other nations and used in international transactions. In effect, the system extended to the US unlimited credit with other nations.

There were some danger signs: growth was uneven.

The Keynesian Success Story

In Britain, Keynes's theory inspired a style of social-democratic government adopted by the post-war Labour Party. Social-democratic policies, such as nationalization of major industries, public health and social welfare services, and close cooperation with unions, have been implemented in other European countries, Sweden, West Germany, etc., not directly influenced by Keynes. But these elementary forms of social-democratic 'public responsibility' in government do not add up to socialism, by any means. They are just another way of managing capitalism, as Keynes himself had recommended.

In this favorable political and economic context, large capitalist countries maintained high levels of employment (least noticeably in the United States where unemployment at 5 percent during the 1950s, ran at double European rates), and very high growth rates, once more with the partial exception of the United States. Even there, however, the economy operated so much better than in the 1930s that relatively few Americans complained.

The post-war boom not only improved living standards but also financed a welfare state in many European countries. Only the United States, the purest capitalist country, lagged behind Europe's social democrats. Only in 1964 did Congress extend rather incomplete health protection to the elderly and the poor. Unlike other industrial societies, the United States still resists public provision for universal health care.

There were some danger signs: growth was uneven. Southern Italy, Brittany, Scotland, and Northern Ireland remained stubbornly depressed. Women everywhere and blacks in the United States gained less than white males. The European miracle drew heavily upon "guest workers" from Yugoslavia, Italy, Turkey, and Spain. At the first breath of recession, host countries shipped home these second-class noncitizens. Thus, measured unemployment rates in prospering western Europe were much lower than in the United States because the Europeans were in a better position than the Americans to export their unemployment.

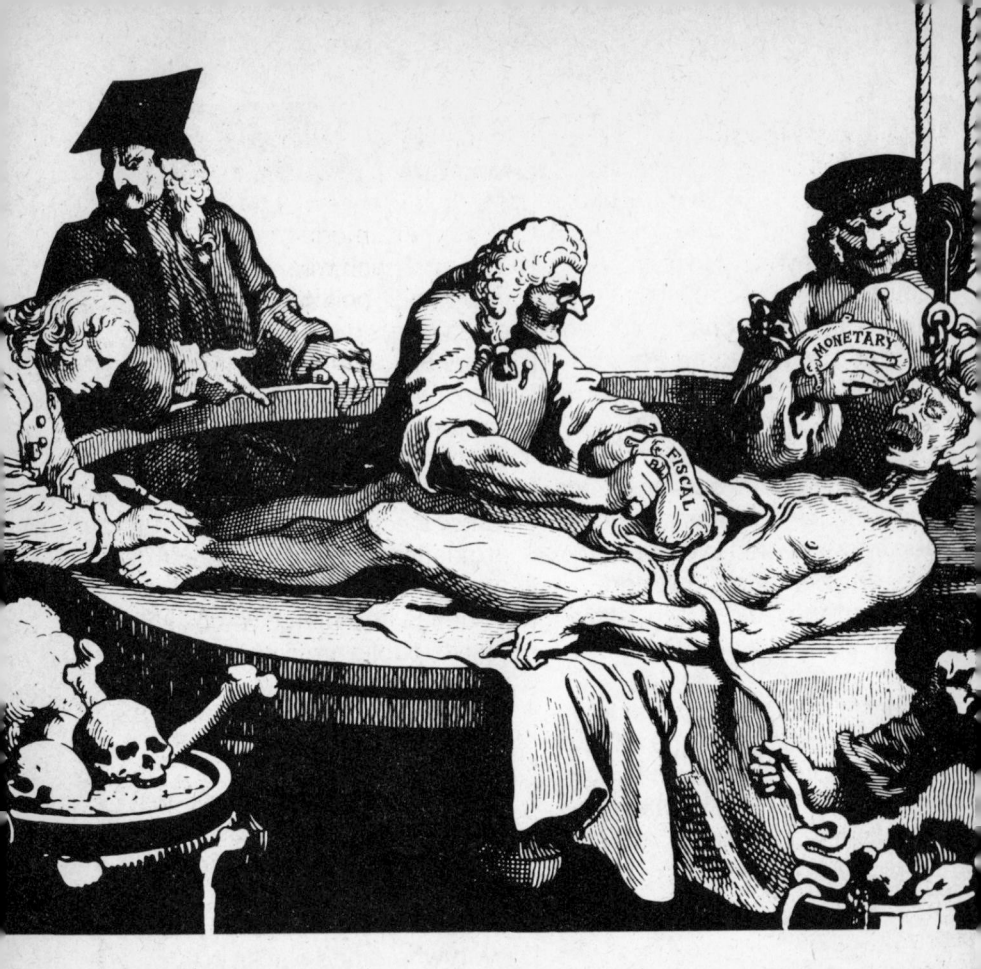

Keynes gave politicians and mainstream economists, particularly in the English-speaking world, confidence that firm management of the economy could tame the business cycle, maintain high employment, and avert the suffering of recession. These economists tended to ignore Keynes's endorsement of egalitarian redistribution and social control of investment. They concentrated upon:

* **Monetary policy** – variations in interest rates and the supply of money designed during recession to stimulate investment and during boom to check inflationary tendencies and

* **Fiscal policy** – tax cuts and increments to public spending calculated in their way to stimulate spending and employment.

As it seemed to cheerful Keynesians in the 1950s and 1960s, all that was required to keep market economies on a smooth course of noninflationary growth and steady improvement in general standards of life was a capacity to fiddle astutely with the supply of money and the national budget – monetary and fiscal policy. It was simply a matter of making certain that private investors spent enough on new machines and factories, or that, as needed, government made good any shortfall in the plans of the private sector.

In the US, confidence in Keynesianism did not extend to the acceptance of a social-democratic mode of government. The approach was economic rather than political. American Keynesians interpreted the apparent success of the 1964 tax cut in their country in stimulating accelerated growth and diminished unemployment as impressive validation of a fiscal policy's efficacy. During the mid-1960s, American economists were more euphoric than they ever had been. In 1966, Walter Heller, President Kennedy's chief economic adviser, delivered this glowing accolade to Keynesian policy:

Economics has come of age in the 1960s. Two presidents have recognized and drawn on modern economics as a source of national strength and Presidential power . . . The paralyzing grip of economic myth and false fears on policy has been loosened, perhaps even broken. We at last accept in fact what was accepted in law twenty years ago . . . that the Federal government has an overreaching responsibility for the nation's economic stability and growth. And we have at last unleashed fiscal and monetary policy for the aggressive pursuits of those objectives.

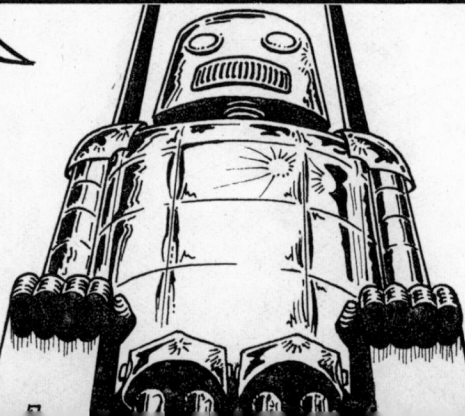

107

How Long Can Affluence Last?

The boom years encouraged politicians and economists in the firm belief that Keynes had solved the problems of capitalism. Affluence encouraged ordinary people in the First World to rely on prosperity as the responsibility of government, social-democratic or not. The apparent success of the Keynesian formula created very high expectations. High incomes, health, social insurance, education, are the benefits of 'reformed' capitalism which many still enjoy today. Such benefits, particularly the public services of the Welfare State, were premised on certain political, as well as economic, conditions: on a collective bargain between capital (including the state) and labour, and a post-war confidence in mass, consensus democracy. For thirty years, people have been encouraged by representative democracy to ask for what they want, have become used to having it, and will become very annoyed if they are now denied it. Public welfare, we are now being told, cannot be extended if it cannot be paid for.

The conditions on which the political consensus was based are now passing. Increasing prosperity is no longer certain; the bargain between labour, capital and the state has broken down; the dominant order is challenged by the underprivileged, immigrants, women and the young; and there is disagreement between the political and economic factions of the élite itself.

The first signs of weakness in the Keynesian strategy began to appear in the late 60s.

The End Of The Boom

Throughout the 1950s and 60s, Western Europe (except Britain) and Japan enjoyed higher growth rates than the US. Throughout the 60s, the US had the lowest productivity growth of all the Western countries. By the mid-sixties the technological gap between the US and its chief rivals was narrowing, in part due to the transfer of technology made possible by the presence of American multinationals within competing economies.

From the late 1950s onwards, the US ran a huge balance of payments deficit with its allies and trade rivals. In the early years the deficit was due to the combined cost of military bases abroad and foreign wars – notably Vietnam – and of financing the enormous investment needs of American multinationals' foreign subsidiaries. Between 1958 and 1970, US corporate investment in the EEC alone grew from $1 billion to $13 billion.

But from the early 60s on, the US foreign trade surplus was not enough to cover the deficit on overall payments abroad – the US ran a large and persistent trade deficit. By 1971, the US had a total overseas dollar deficit of $50 billion, more than four times the size of its gold reserves, which had shrunk to less than half their post-war level. Those outstanding dollars represented a huge loan extended to the US – a loan without interest, with no sign of repayment, and with every sign of growing as the Vietnam war dragged on.

European economies were being flooded with surplus US dollars, as American merchandise became less and less competitive and more and more overpriced in export markets. These surplus dollars threatened to become a source of European inflation and they also placed the World Bank and the International Monetary Fund under increasing pressure. These Bretton Woods institutions used the American dollar as their major asset. All during the 1950s and 60s, the United States linked its paper dollars to gold by promising other governments (though not American citizens) that they could at any time redeem dollars at a guaranteed price in gold – one ounce of gold for every $35.

As the volume of currency in the growing Eurodollar market ballooned, that promise became decreasingly credible. **Eurodollars** are ordinary dollars controlled by foreigners, foreign governments, or American corporations operating in Europe.

Military expenditure in the mid-60's had helped the U.S. economy to its fastest growth rates for many years.

The Vietnam War

By 1968 the Vietnam war had long ceased to be a boon for the American economy, let alone the American people (and the Vietnamese). Military expenditure in the mid-1960s had helped the US economy to its fastest growth rates and lowest unemployment levels for many years. But this expenditure had moved to the point where it began to cut into profit margins. Taxes, interest rates and raw material costs rose as government demands on resources expanded to pay for the war.

The Vietnam war sowed the seeds of **stagflation**, an ugly and intractable combination of inflation and unemployment. Escalated by stealth, the Vietnam war attracted the opposition of growing numbers of Americans. For that reason, and also because President Lyndon Johnson feared Congressional curtailment of Great Society programs addressed to education, poverty, health, job training and low income housing, his administration concealed the true cost of a dreadful war, refrained until 1967 from seeking new taxes to finance it, and allowed a **demand-pull inflation** to begin.

Demand-pull inflation occurs whenever the number of dollars in the hands of consumers and the business community exceeds at existing prices the dollar value of saleable merchandise and services. Stores mark up their prices, unions press for cost of living increases, and since business is good, their employers grant them, pass the increases on to customers in still higher prices, and set off a second round of wage demands.

Demand-pull inflation is accompanied by **cost-push** pressure which occurs whenever monopolies and oligopolies push up prices even in recessions, much preferring smaller sales at larger unit profits to larger sales at smaller unit profits.

As **The Economist** put it late in 1968: "Some time ago Wall Street switched from its original view that the war was pepping up a tired boom to thinking that it is aggravating every problem of the economy and forcing restrictive action (tax increases and above all tight money and high interest rates) that investors emphatically dislike. Peace, the Street now thinks, would be the best thing that could happen." (26 October 1968)

It became increasingly clear that only a true depression of several years duration could halt inflation.

Nixon's Planned Recession

By the time Richard Nixon succeeded Lyndon Johnson as President of the United States in January 1969, the danger of inflation was sufficiently acute to persuade Mr. Nixon to opt for a planned recession. As the new President soon discovered, recessions work poorly to extinguish inflation both because monopolists and oligopolists continue to mark up their prices even as they lose sales, and because the stronger unions protect their members by insisting on cost of living protection even at the cost of some layoffs. It became increasingly clear that only a true depression of several years duration could halt inflation.

Panicked at the prospect of running for re-election in 1972 in the middle of a recession, Mr. Nixon abruptly reversed his field, discarded long-standing opposition to controls, and on August 15, 1971 clamped a 90-day freeze on wages and most prices. After the freeze expired, the President instituted looser Phase II restraints upon both profits and wages.

What impressed Americans were the freeze and the controls. For the world economy, the President's most fateful step was *de facto* devaluation of the American dollar. In the jargon of finance, Mr. Nixon slammed shut the gold window by informing all holders of gold that the United States Treasury would no longer buy gold at $35 per glittering ounce.

The dollar was set free to "float" in value. Its price in lira, francs, pounds, and yen became a matter of supply and demand on the part of people who wanted dollars and others disposed to get rid of them. Very soon the same American dollar which in the 1950s traded for four West German marks could be exchanged for less than two.

The ending of fixed exchange rates turned out to be disastrous for capitalism. It meant the ending of two decades of certainty, and the start of a new era of instability, violent currency fluctuations and long term recession.

The oil import bills of the First World simultaneously stimulate inflation and recession.

114

Inflation And The Energy Crisis

In the space of weeks in the winter of 1973-4, OPEC more than quadrupled the world price of petroleum. Oil does many things besides run autos and heat houses and flats. As a raw material, it is a vital ingredient of chemical fertilizers, plastics, synthetic fibers, and pharmaceuticals, among a good deal else. The American oil import bill in 1980 was estimated at a figure between $80 and $100 billion, between three and four percent of the Gross National Product.

This massive new claim by OPEC on the resources of western Europe, Japan, and the United States also resembles a tax. After paying for gasoline, home heating fuel, and the other energy-related items they need, consumers have less income left to buy other things. National leaders then face an unpalatable choice. They can encourage their central bankers to create enough money so that the public can continue to buy, or try to buy, as much as before oil prices escalated; or presidents and prime ministers can urge central bankers to cut down on the creation of new money.

If they opt for the first and easier choice, they promote inflation as consumers and businessmen drive up the prices of output which has increased less rapidly in amount than the new money made available to them. Recession and loss of political popularity are the consequences of the second choice, monetary restraint.

In practice, politicians veer uneasily back and forth between the two calamities. In the United States, this instability of national policy has contributed to the persistence of **stagflation** – a mixture of high inflation and persistent unemployment. France, Switzerland, West Germany, and Japan have conserved money more effectively than the United States. They have also succeeded in restraining money growth and raising interest rates without dangerously adding to domestic unemployment by ruthlessly packing off foreign workers. Moreover, OPEC oil continues to be priced in American dollars. German marks, French francs, and Japanese yen since 1973 have purchased increasing numbers of dollars as American currency has declined in relation to other major trading media of exchange. Accordingly OPEC oil has been cheaper in Germany or Japan than in the United States. Although the dollar has lost credibility as a reserve currency, no acceptable substitute has emerged.

Should We Blame OPEC For Inflation?

Oil tends to get muddled up with the Middle East conflict. But there is more to it than that. One has to consider the spectacular rise of multinational banking. Western and in particular American banks are exercising growing economic power on an international scale. They can deploy resources across national boundaries and back again, leaving national governments helpless and bemused.

One of the most significant effects of the 1973 fourfold increase in the price of oil and the ensuing slump was the spectacular increase in the wealth and power of multinational banks. Since 1974 there has been a huge increase in the money capital flowing into the coffers of this vast, integrated global banking system. It is outside the control of any government, and is dominated by a few dozen giant banks that transact business in every corner of the world. The offshore Eurodollars, Euromarks and other 'stateless' currencies that they are able to hurl across national boundaries 24 hours a day amount to at least 400 billion dollars – in money terms ten times more than a decade ago, and four times more than in 1972.

The last boom (1972-1973) saw grave shortages of almost every type of raw material, a shortage made extreme by the instability of currencies which obliges traders to move out of unreliable cash into commodities as soon as possible. It was a brief boom – before long the slump had destroyed the demand for the exports of the Less Developed Countries. But the slump did not end the inflation in the manufactured exports of the More Developed Countries (the imports of the Less Developed Countries); nor did it prevent the increase in the price of oil which afflicted the imports of many Third World countries which do not produce oil.

The majority of the world's countries moved into massive trade deficit. Western private banks, faced with a contraction of borrowing in the First World as a result of the recession, were only too eager to provide short-term loans to the Less Developed Countries and Eastern Europe to sustain their own profits. The loans were used in part to finance industrial imports from the More Developed Countries, which helped keep up demand, and made them more dependent on exports to the Third World.

This resurgence of finance capital is fuelled by the petrodollars being recycled through the multinational banks in the Euromarkets by the oil producing states. In 1980, the OPEC surplus will reach $180 billion.

But instability is the corollary of the new power and size of leading banks, for OPEC controls many of their assets and many of their loans are shaky.

PAYMENTS BALANCES (CURRENT ACCOUNT)

	Industrialized Countries	Non-oil developing countries
	$bn	$bn
1974	− 12.2	− 36.9
1975	+ 16.2	− 45.8
1976	− 2.8	− 32.1
1977	− 6.6	− 28.0
1978	+ 29.6	− 36.2
1979	− 10.0	− 54.9
1980 (est)	− 47.5	− 68.0
1981 (est)	− 20.0	−100.0

The volume of Third World indebtedness soared, and the cost of servicing the debt interest payments and repayments, threatens to strangle efforts at development. Some 29 countries account for 70 percent of the debt, and a much smaller group for the major part of this – particularly Brazil, Mexico, Argentina, Peru, Zaire, South Korea and the Philippines, most of them among the fastest growing Less Developed Countries.

In 1979 OPEC accumulated a $60 billion balance of payments surplus, an aseptic way to say that OPEC sold to the rest of the

World $60 billion more than its members bought from other countries. Some of the money came from developing societies like India, Pakistan, Zaire, Tanzania, Peru, Turkey, and Brazil which possess almost no oil of their own and limited resources to finance a rising energy bill.

OPEC countries spent much of their earnings on western technology, construction, and consumer goods. They also deposited tens of billions of dollars in American and European banks and proceeded to use a portion of them to acquire real estate, corporate and government securities, and the voting stock of major corporations such as Krupp and Mercedes-Benz in West Germany and their counterparts in the rest of Europe and the United States.

Major money market banks such as Chase Manhattan, Morgan Guaranty, and Citibank have financed the oil import bills of Third World countries without oil of their own through huge loans made possible by OPEC deposits.

The question is how long the arrangement can endure. Western banks are increasingly uneasy about continuing to lend ever larger sums to weak and politically unstable states like Zaire and Turkey. They worry about the larger and larger percentage of export earnings required simply to pay interest on debt.

their own bankruptcy. Already there have been some temporary defaults or very near risks – in Zaire, Peru, Argentina, North Korea, Indonesia, Egypt, and South Korea. This is why the International Monetary Fund, the First World's central bank, set up to offset sudden payments crises, is being vastly expanded to supervise borrowing countries, using its lending powers to force governments to cut imports and raise exports. Argentina and Zaire have both had their debts 'reorganized' by the IMF, and it has supervised Mexico, Brazil and even Britain. Brazil followed a policy of deliberately pushing up its debts so that the lending banks would be too committed to allow it to default, and would carry on recycling the loans. When the US intervened to limit South Korea's massive borrowings, Seoul promptly turned to West German banks to raise the cash.

Some of the US and European banks have become very much exposed to the risk of default, and so to the possible precipitation of

In 1967 some 28 percent of the total Third World debt – about 12 billion dollars – was owed to private sources; by 1976, an estimated 40 percent was owed to private sources – about 75 billion dollars, of which 45 billion was owed to US banks. Apart from US banks, German banks have risen to prominence in the period of vast expansion of the Eurocurrency market. Of the top ten banks in the Eurobond market in 1978, the two leaders were both West German. British banks, mainly Lloyds and Barclays, and most recently Japanese banks, have also launched themselves as multinational financiers.

In the richer countries themselves, the realization grows that living standards must probably fall or at best grow with excruciating sluggishness because OPEC has staked its claim on western Gross National Product. The United States' 1980 oil import bill, some $80-$100 billion, will probably exceed 3 percent of the year's GNP.

There is a second fragile link in the financial transmission chain. On either political or economic grounds, key OPEC producers might withdraw large deposits from major banks in the west and trigger financial panic and, far from incidentally, abruptly halt lending to the poorer members of the Third World.

Partly because of domestic inflation, partly because of the adverse impact of Vietnam on American productivity, the growth of the American economy, which had been sluggish in comparison with European and Japanese performers since 1945, began still more to lag and the capacity of American exports to compete with their major rivals even more to erode.

As controls were relaxed at the start of 1973, inflation spurted anew. Thus, even before OPEC's dramatic intervention in October 1973, an era of comparatively stable post-World War II capitalist prosperity was drawing to a conclusion. By no special coincidence, the diminishing efficacy of Keynesian economic policy, demonstrated by the simultaneous appearance of inflation and unemployment, stimulated an alternative intellectual response among economists in England, France, West Germany and the United States. This is **monetarism**.

The End Of A Keynesian Era

The capitalist world now faces a crisis that should never have happened — that Keynesian techniques and social-democratic government policies were supposed to banish forever. During the boom years, economic prosperity became identified with Keynesian-style government. But Keynesian demand management seems unable to deal with the simultaneous appearance of inflation and unemployment. So it is not surprising that the reputation of governments for successful economic management has fallen.

Is Keynesianism finished? Is there an alternative economic response? Milton Friedman, the intellectual guru of monetarism, thinks so.

The failure of Western governments to achieve their proclaimed objectives has produced a widespread reaction against big government. In Britain the reaction swept Margaret Thatcher to power in 1979 on a platform pledging her Conservative government to reverse the socialist policies that had been followed by both Labour and earlier Conservative governments ever since the end of World War II. In Sweden in 1976, the reaction led to the defeat of the Social Democratic party after more than four decades of uninterrupted rule. In France the reaction led to a dramatic change in policy designed to eliminate government control of prices and wages and sharply reduce other forms of government intervention. In the United States the reaction has been manifested most dramatically in the tax revolt that has swept the nation, symbolized by the passage of Proposition 13 in California, and realized in a number of states in constitutional amendments limiting state taxes.

After Keynes, What?

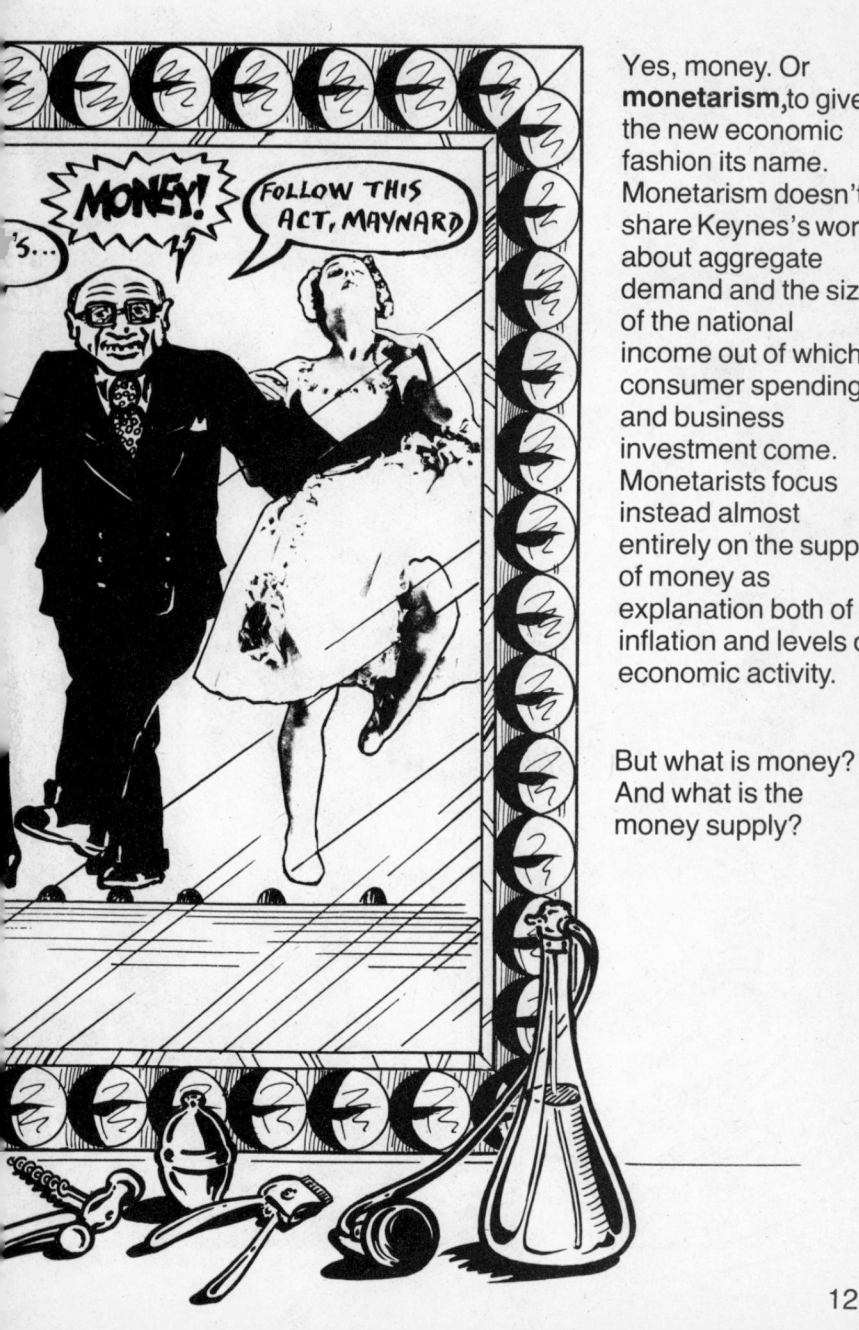

Yes, money. Or **monetarism,** to give the new economic fashion its name. Monetarism doesn't share Keynes's worry about aggregate demand and the size of the national income out of which consumer spending and business investment come. Monetarists focus instead almost entirely on the supply of money as explanation both of inflation and levels of economic activity.

But what is money? And what is the money supply?

Money Counts

Money consists of paper currency plus the kind of deposits in banks on which checks can be written. In all advanced industrial societies, the second kind of money is far more important than the first.

Governments control the amount of money of both kinds through their central banks – the Bank of England, the Bundesbank, the American Federal Reserve. Central bankers operate by increasing or decreasing the reserves to be held against their deposits by commercial banks such as Barclays or Chase Manhattan. The techniques are intricate in detail but simple in principle. When, for example, the Federal Reserve wishes to enlarge the amount of money in circulation, it buys some of the hundreds of billions of dollars of government bonds and notes owned by individuals, commercial banks, corporations, pension and mutual funds, life insurers, and others. If Chase Manhattan sells $1 million in federal bonds to Federal Reserve, it gets a check for that amount. **This is new money**. Chase lends it promptly (less a percentage it must hold on deposit in the Federal Reserve) to businessmen and consumers.

The borrowers increase their checking deposits by the amounts they have borrowed.

This is more new money. As they write checks on their accounts, the people who receive them put them in their checking accounts and **more new money is created**. If banks are legally required to keep a 20 percent reserve against deposits, $1 million of new money generated by the initial sale will eventually create a total $5 million of added money, as banks receive new deposits, make new loans, and enlarge the volume of outstanding checking account money.

Monetarists assert the existence of a direct link between the rate at which the supply of money grows and the pace of inflation. Whenever central banks enlarge the money supply by a percentage greater than growth in the output of the goods and services, prices rise. Conversely, if a central bank were to add only 5 percent to the money supply while output was increasing at a 10 percent rate, then prices inevitably would decline.

It follows that communities which aim at price stability must instruct their central bankers to abide by a firm rule: the money supply must increase at the same rate as output rises. No faster, no slower.

Another golden rule of monetarism is that government should mind its own business and not interfere in private economic decisions taken in the free market. But what is the business of government?

Balance the budget at all times; keep central bankers on good behaviour; cut social expenditures. These policies will stimulate investment, promote economic growth, tame inflation and restore capitalism's dynamism.

You want the national economy to stay healthy?
Keep out of it!

What do monetarists say to people worried about economic instability, employment and income?

Save more and spend less!

Mrs Thatcher interpreted her 1979 election victory as a mandate to shrink social spending and shift the incidence of tax burdens from progressive levies on income to regressive sales taxes. Her doubling of the Value Added Tax (VAT) imposes heavier burdens as one slides down the income slope. The best way to avoid VAT or any other sales tax is to save more and spend less. This course of action is closely correlated with income position. To be rich is to save without pain. To be poor is to spend every pound and pay tax on the lot.

Common Market countries all levy VAT, and the notion has attracted support in American circles, including the former Chairman of the major Congressional tax-writing committees, Senator Russell Long and Representative Al Ullman. Conservative Americans advance the same justifications of VAT as their English colleagues. Saving should be encouraged. The way to go is to reduce the progression in the personal income tax and by so doing encourage people to save more money, take larger investment chances, and, in the end, reap the rewards of their courage.

In Britain, as in France, West Germany and the USA, monetarists tell the same story with different accents.

> Taxes which now finance health care, pensions for the elderly, unemployed, and disabled, and other items of the welfare state agenda are heavy burdens upon employers and their young, productive workers. If only benefits were curtailed, payroll taxes could easily be reduced, business costs commensurately diminished, and profits and growth stimulated.

Under the disguise of providing incentives to individual effort and investment, monetarists are systematically depriving social programs, health protection and education. In Britain, even that once sacred cow, the British Broadcasting System, is being ''cut back''.

Monetarism is the respectable economic excuse for removing protections and benefits extracted painfully from unwilling governments after decades of struggle by the labour movements.

Of course, monetarist policy isn't that simple: it can command the sophisticated techniques of modern economics.
But are the critics correct who accuse monetarism of being a retrogressive, reactionary throwback to Adam Smith and laissez-faire economics?

the positive state of liberty is indiv

Security of property and contract, free competition, stable money ounds good!

Conservatism, under the Iron Lady, Maggie Thatcher, won over a section of the working-class electorate who were fed up with the Keynesian policies of a social-democratic Labour government. Thatcher stands as a populist champion against the burden of taxation, welfare scroungers, the inefficiency of nationalized industries, the threat to public order posed by immigrants, unions, students and other minority groups.

Positively, monetarism stands for a return to a liberal society.

Thatcher's 1979 election triumph over the Labour Party was seen as a great victory of monetarist common sense over social democracy. The political and economic forces underpinning Labour are social-democratic and Keynesian, not 'socialist', and not as formidable as Conservatives pretend.

The real questions are: what does the triumph of monetarism mean? is it temporary? and why was it so easy to topple Keynesianism?

Left Reactions To Monetarism

The Left, in England and elsewhere, believes that monetarism is a return to old-fashioned, 19th century laissez-faire economics. Laissez-faire is simply not relevant to today's form of capitalism, that is, to the problems of monopoly or corporate capitalism.

On present British evidence, social democrats seem better at running modern capitalism than monetarists.

Then why aren't they in power now?

Crisis has to be policed — as well as managed.

Other leftists see Thatcher's monetarist policies as a means of strengthening the state's forces of repression. The state spends less on welfare and more on maintaining law and order in a rough time of recession and crisis.

This much is clear. Monetarism is a return to the fundamentals of capitalism. It is a mistake to think these fundamentals are simply "old-fashioned". They have deep roots in capitalist society, even today. Keynesianism, too, did not cut itself off from those roots: it was, and remains, a mode of capitalist management.

So why has orthodox Keynesian policy been replaced by a monetarist one? What would Keynes himself say, if he came back to visit Milton Friedman?

IN GOD WE TRUST
THE REST PAY CASH

First point: the idea that inflation can be traced to an over-expansion of the money supply by governments has long been held by conservative economists and politicians.

Every government today is forced to accept monetarism if they wish to maintain the confidence of the international finance markets.

Take the example of the British Labour government, recently defeated by Thatcher. It was monetarist. It eased the burden on corporations (which raises profits but doesn't contribute to aggregate demand) and at the same time cut state expenditure.

Didn't I say that aggregate demand **has** to be maintained by government spending on roads, dams, whatever?

I know. But we've got to cut government spending to keep the IMF happy!

The price of running a welfare state — and at the same time maintaining external confidence in the currency — means that social democrats have a price to pay. They have to reduce the domestic rate of inflation by restricting the money supply.

In other words, what the monetarists prescribe for the money supply, taxation and public expenditure is a well-known, orthodox deflationary policy.

The real difference between social democrats and monetarists is something else. For the monetarist, controlling the money supply is the **only** obligation of government; some social democrats, however, believe that this is only one more technique in managing the national economy.

How is a government supposed to deal with employment, national economic growth and the exchange rate for currency?

That's not a government's responsibility. The market will see to that.

Monetarists are great believers in the free market. But even that isn't new – or even purely monetarist. Since 1945 there has been a debate among European social democrats whether to follow the path of the market or government planning. Social democrats in the British Labour Party prefer a social welfare or 'mixed' economy and accept government planning. This is sometimes called the collectivist version of social democracy. But there is also a liberal version. In Germany, the Social Democratic Party supports a liberal, market economy.

I DON'T CARE WHICH SYSTEM WE HAVE, SO LONG AS I CAN MAKE SOME MONEY

Monetarism does radically break with the goals of Keynesian economic management, and, of course, with social-democratic government.

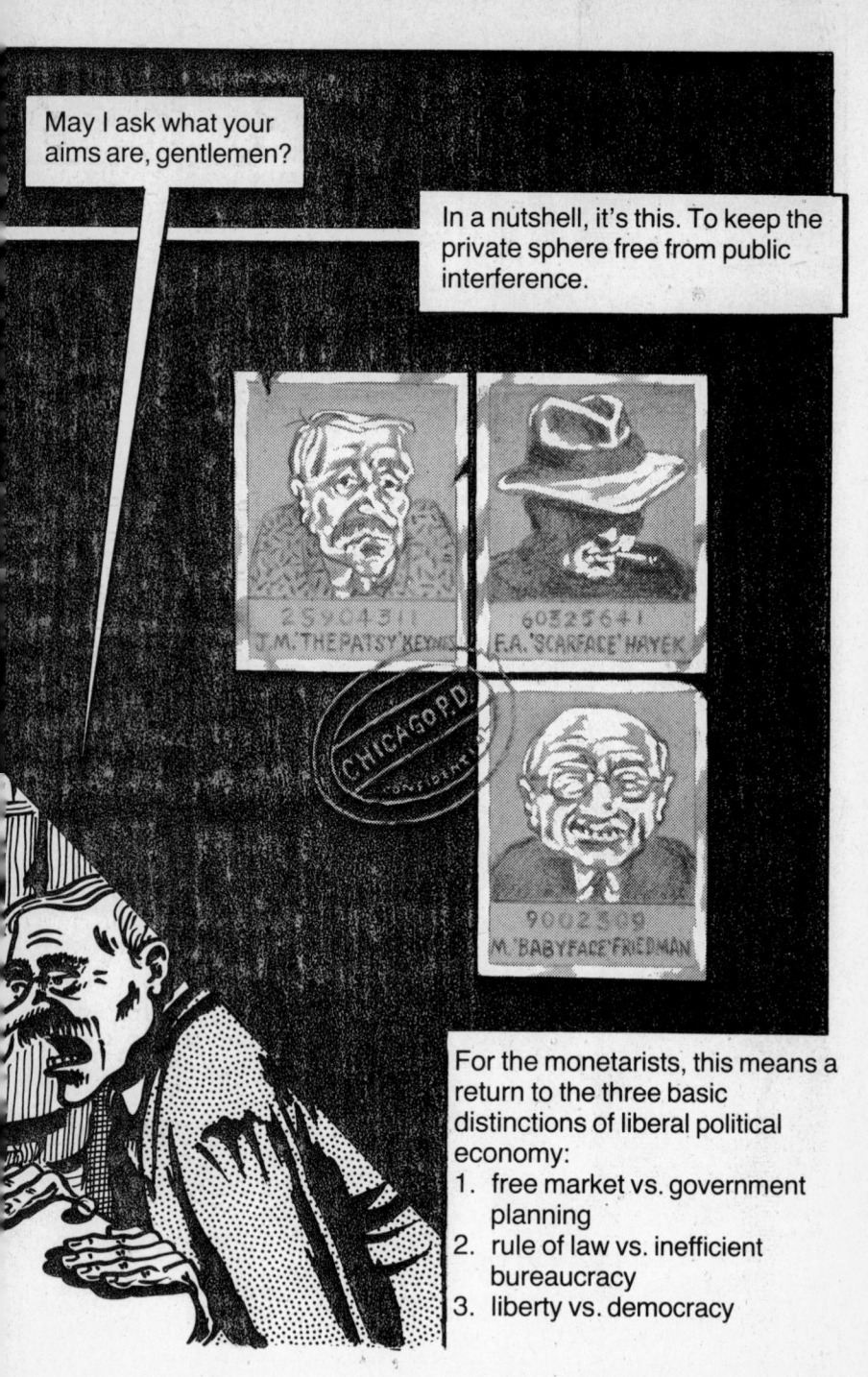

May I ask what your aims are, gentlemen?

In a nutshell, it's this. To keep the private sphere free from public interference.

For the monetarists, this means a return to the three basic distinctions of liberal political economy:
1. free market vs. government planning
2. rule of law vs. inefficient bureaucracy
3. liberty vs. democracy

1. The Free Market

Monetarists attack the Keynesian idea that government should be responsible for national economic expansion and prosperity. The state has to pay for defence, but, apart from that, its main duty is a sound monetary policy.

Government shouldn't mess around with the market system of competitive private industry.

The market will always supply goods at a much lower cost than the state.

What are you going to do about unemployment?

Nothing. That's not a matter for political concern or government intervention.

Unemployment is the fault of unions who won't adapt themselves to the market.

Monetarists do not accept the blame for low wages, poverty, demoralization, uprooted communities and lost industries. Keith Joseph, the present Secretary of Industry, told the shipbuilding workers on Clydeside faced with redundancy . . .

100,000 workers change jobs in Britain every week. You'll have to do the same!

With more than 15 million unemployed in the major capitalist countries, the monetarist outlook helps governments and electorates to accept permanent high levels of unemployment.

Obsession with the market, free competition and freedom from the state has encouraged the popular belief that monetarism stands for the protection of enterprising small businesses and control over private monopolies. The idea that individual effort and skill will find its reward in the free market is typical of Maggie Thatcher's populism.

Cockles 'n mussels – get out there 'n hustle!

She doesn't really believe that, surely?

But the market isn't moral: it is as likely to reward luck and status as skill and effort. What do monetarists say about that?

Ask the market to be fair? Forget it.

Another Nobel Prize-winning monetarist, F.A. Hayek, openly admits that a society based on a free market will constantly create unmerited, unfair opportunities and rewards. But he justifies this by pointing to the general benefits everyone receives from a maximizing of opportunities for industrial exchange and choice.

British and American monetarists, like Hayek, justify corporate capitalism and do not see any need for the market to defend the interests of small business and consumers.

Hayek believes that anti-monopoly interventions by governments are, in the long run, worse than monopolies themselves. But monetarists don't accept that unions have the same rights as corporate monopolies.

2. The Law Versus Unions

Other pro-corporate, capitalist economists would nowadays defend the role of unions as necessary for efficient planning. Some monetarists agree; but most of them don't. They blame the unions for exercising the wrong sort of monopoly, which has a bad effect on the market, including the labour market itself.

British and American monetarists "regard monopoly powers of unions in the labour markets as the principal reason for growing government regulation of the economy and lax monetary policy. This is because trade unions 'distort' relative prices in the labour market, making many activities unprofitable that would otherwise be profitable, so creating unemployment; and they impede the introduction of new technology, so reducing mobility and freezing the pattern of employment whilst the pattern of demand is shifting. The economy performs less well than it should, and governments under pressure to retain and win votes intervene in private industry to try to make it more efficient, and expand demand to reduce unemployment. This creates inflation which keeps the economy prosperous for a while at the expense of making the final crash and the scale of reorganization more extensive." ANDREW GAMBLE

But monetarists do not hold unions directly responsible for inflation. Wage rises can cause inflation only if the government **allows** the money supply to increase to finance higher prices. Unions are blamed, however, for unemployment, stagnation and strikes which afflict the market.

Milton Friedman's Nobel lecture puts the monetarist position clearly: unemployment only exists because wage rates don't fall far enough.

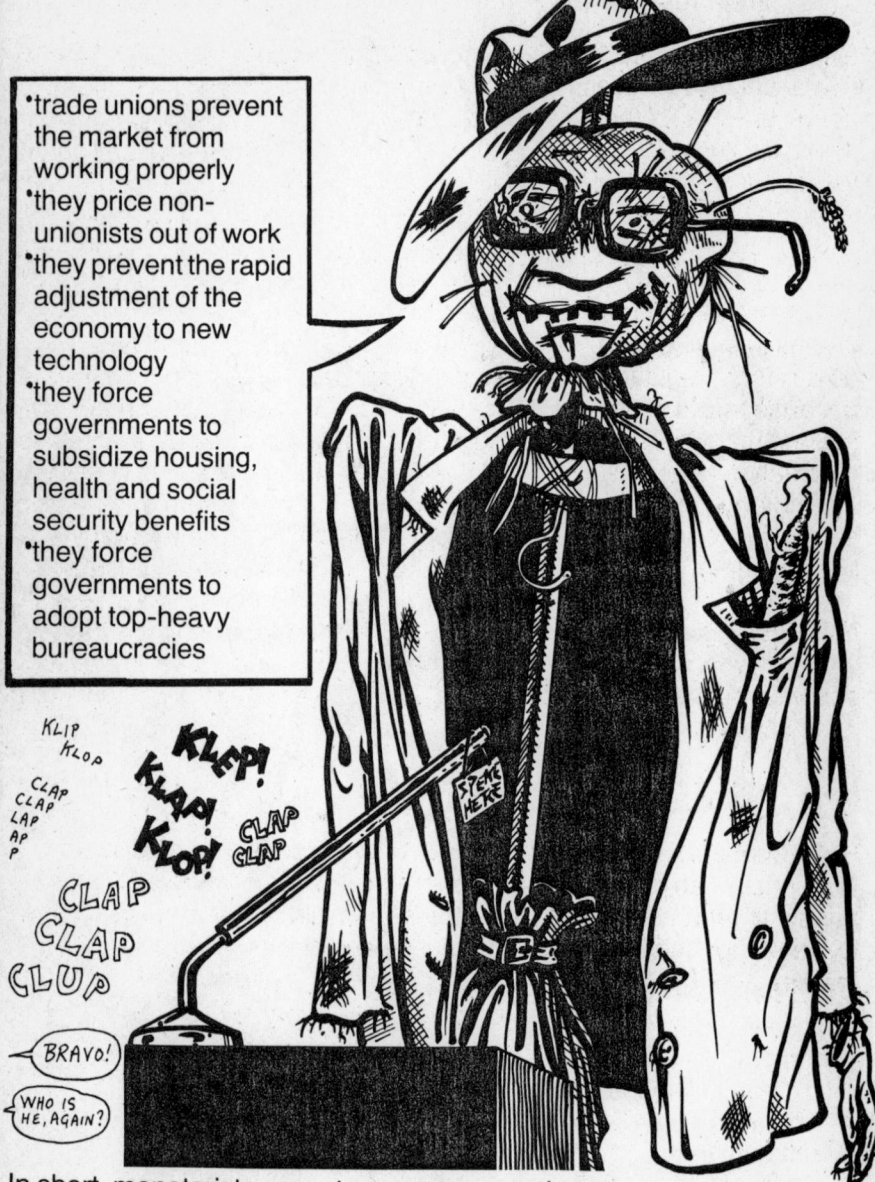

- trade unions prevent the market from working properly
- they price non-unionists out of work
- they prevent the rapid adjustment of the economy to new technology
- they force governments to subsidize housing, health and social security benefits
- they force governments to adopt top-heavy bureaucracies

In short, monetarists cannot see any economic reason at all for the existence of unions.

Unions are a strain and a drag on the market – and the strongest legal measures are justified in being used against them in the public interest. In Britain in 1968, the Conservative politician Enoch Powell argued that union power rested on three legal privileges . . .

1. picketing – the freedom to intimidate
2. freedom to impose costs with impunity
3. immunity from actions of tort

With a Conservative government now in power in Britain, we can see monetarism in legal action against the privileges of organized labour. If Thatcher's attack on the powers of unions is successful, what will be the economic outcome?

Simple. A solution to the age-old problem of labour supply in capitalist society.

That is: the right labour, in the right quantity at the right price.

3. Liberty Isn't Only Democracy

Monetarists blame unions for interfering with the individual liberty of workers and employers. But what do they mean exactly by 'liberty'? F.A. Hayek has spelled it out clearly.

Hayek defines liberty as "that condition of men in which coercion of some by others is reduced as much as possible in society."

Sounds reasonable. But is it, really?

In one all-important area, the monetarists say, the state, as a social agency, can reduce coercion by individuals if it is able to punish anyone who breaks the laws governing individual exchange.

But how do you reduce coercion by the state itself?

The rights and activities of private enterprise have to be legally protected from government infringements.

By keeping the private sector free from public interference.

This monetarist notion of liberty is specifically aimed against Keynesian economic management – and against the mass form of representative democracy. Monetarist liberty means that there are many laws which governments should **not** have the power to change. While popular sovereignty, instead, demands that a government elected by the people has the right to overturn and refashion **all** laws.

This is still abstract. What do the monetarists actually propose?

Take the money supply out of the hands of politicians – then you'll have liberty!

Why's that? Because politicians, in their pursuit of mass popularity, are tempted to interfere with the money supply, to satisfy the wishes of the majority at the expense of the budget. Monetarists believe that money should not be subject to democratic pressure. A strictly regulated money supply should be the constraint within which all governments are obliged to operate.

Monetarists look upon politics, too, as a market. And from that angle, democracy suffers from a big flaw. It is this: democracy has no "budget constraint" which limits what the voter can vote for in the way that it limits what the consumer can afford to buy.

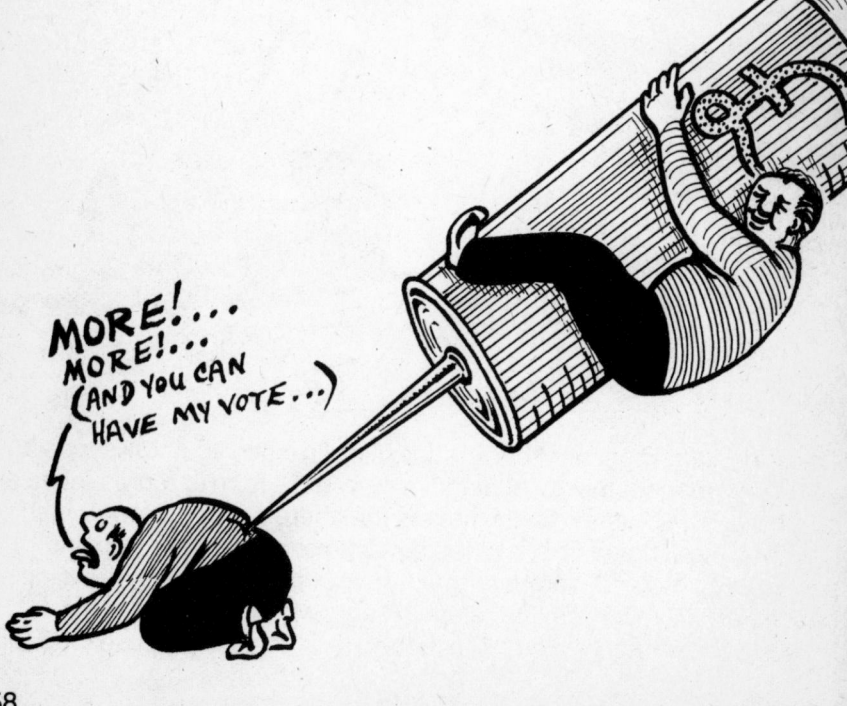

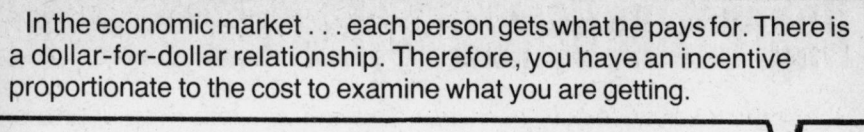

In the economic market . . . each person gets what he pays for. There is a dollar-for-dollar relationship. Therefore, you have an incentive proportionate to the cost to examine what you are getting.

But voters are not obliged to consider costs. And this encourages competitive bidding for votes between the political parties. Democratic governments are led to offer more than they can deliver and to interfere with the private sphere of market relations between individuals – and, hence, to weaken liberty in the name of democracy.

Repressing Democracy

Pinochet's regime in Chile is a nightmare example of "putting democracy on ice". Outright political repression has been applied to cure inflation; murder and terror have been used to protect the "economic freedom" of the market.

Monetarists believe that they are good democrats. They think that their version of economic freedom will in time lead to the restoration of political liberty in Chile. On the evidence, their aid to Pinochet repression has simply strengthened dictatorship.

PINOCHET WITH ARGENTINA'S DICTATOR VIDELLA

Monetarism's one message is simple, loud and clear: the market is the best, most efficient way of satisfying our material needs because it is based on freedom of exchange which guarantees maximum individual choice and minimum measurable costs. But monetarists do not include **social** costs in their profit and loss accounts.

What happens to social justice in your market scheme?

It has to look after itself.

Don't be such a sentimental slob, Maynard.

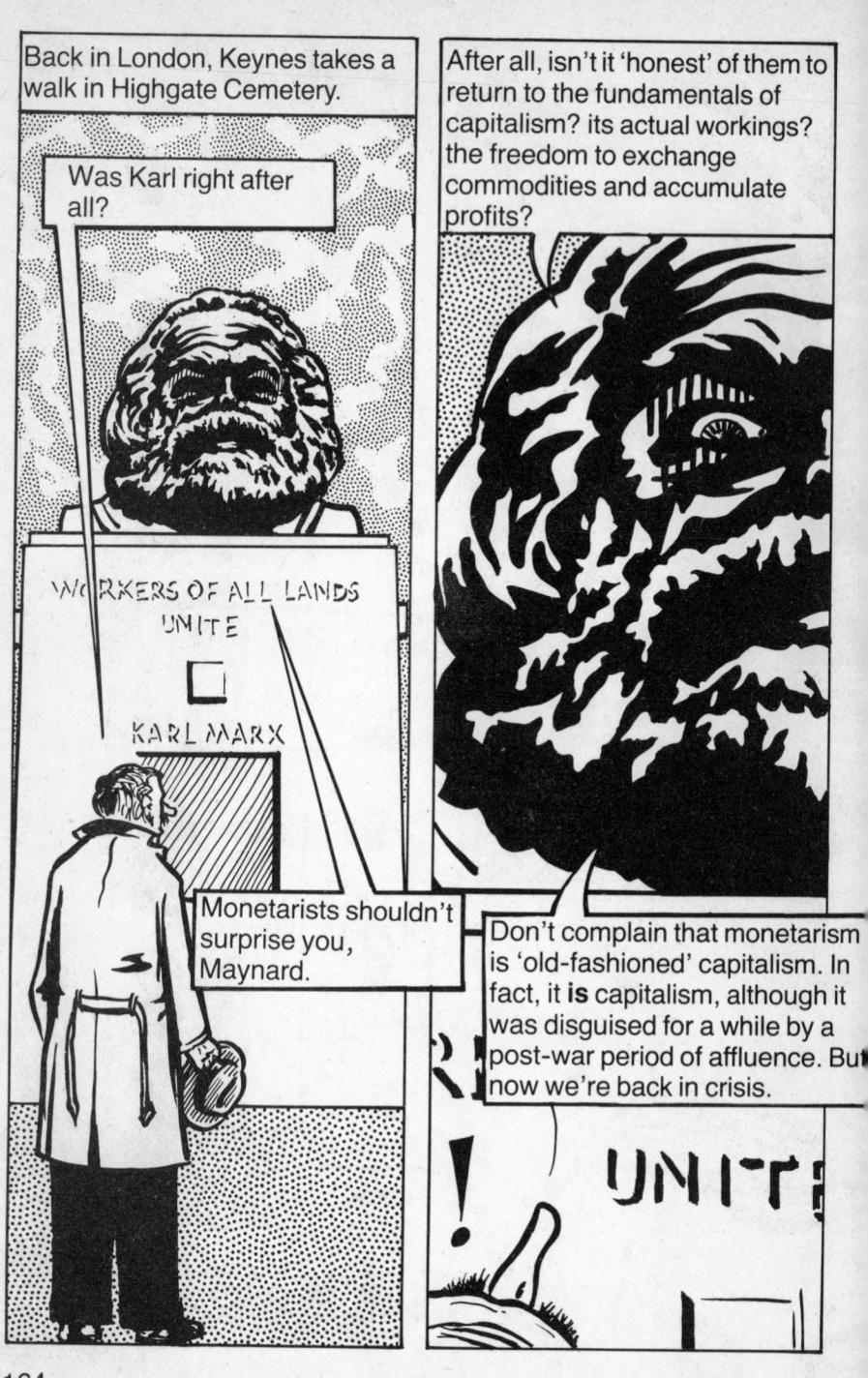

 is the full-page comic. The following is the text contained in its panels:

Back in London, Keynes takes a walk in Highgate Cemetery.

Was Karl right after all?

After all, isn't it 'honest' of them to return to the fundamentals of capitalism? its actual workings? the freedom to exchange commodities and accumulate profits?

WORKERS OF ALL LANDS UNITE

KARL MARX

Monetarists shouldn't surprise you, Maynard.

Don't complain that monetarism is 'old-fashioned' capitalism. In fact, it **is** capitalism, although it was disguised for a while by a post-war period of affluence. But now we're back in crisis.

UNITE!

Monetarists think they can handle the crisis of capitalism by being 'good' capitalists. But they're mistaken about two things.

First, on the level of theory. They describe the market only in terms of free universal exchange. They don't tell us that the market is transformed by capital accumulation. You see, if all persons were merchants and independent producers, the market would be fine. But, in fact, they aren't. Some accumulate, while others do not. So the market is not 'universal' for everyone. And what is the social effect of that?

Socially speaking, the market means that capitalists buy labour and workers sell it. But this really means that a contradiction exists between these two classes of people. Inevitably, there must be a conflict of interest between them. There is, and must always be, a conflict between 'free' individual market choice (the freedom to buy or sell labour) and the collective benefits which each class will seek to consolidate.

Still, I prefer to look at it another way, Karl . . .
Monetarists go wrong because most people are consumers, not savers. And they've now come to

The world's become a lot more complicated since your time, Karl. In the industrial world, we've gotten used to abundance.

WORKERS OF ALL LANI

Suppose I agreed. That still leaves my second point. Can your economic planning achieve social peace? You'll achieve that only if you manage another boom. But you're paying for the last one – the monetarists are right – in terms of inflation, recession, unemployment, etc., etc. In other words, Maynard, can you solve the problem of the falling rate of profit?

Can **anybody** do that?

You mean, will capitalism survive? Or is there an alternative to it?

Capitalist economy (Keynesian, monetarist or otherwise) is based on certain assumptions:

1. individual calculation and the pursuit of self-interest

2. the accommodation and adjustment of private interests through competition

3. the market forms of exchange, based on commodities, money and the law.

The free market is the capitalist model of social relations. In theory, it is supposed to be the best provision for the material needs and innate rights of humanity.

Is there **another** model?

Finale

1. THE CASE AGAINST CAPITALISM REVIEWED

Modern capitalism originated in the force and fraud which drove the English workers off the land into the factories created by the Industrial Revolution. The magnates who operated the textile mills extracted their profit from the exploitation at first of young children and women and later of adult males.

Even after the inital harshness of industrialism was mitigated by rising real wages, union pressure and social reform, income and wealth continued to be far more inequitably distributed than considerations of efficiency and incentive required. Throughout its history, capitalism has been an unstable, disorderly mode of organization in which business cycles have periodically disrupted the lives of workers and bankrupted farmers and small businessmen.

Even in the eyes of its defenders, capitalism has been deficient in two additional regards. There are very few competitive markets of the sort envisaged by Adam Smith and his followers. To an increasing degree, capitalist economies are directed by the entirely visible hands of monopolists, multinational giants and domestic oligopolists.

And finally, the argument that competition, even where it is to be found, must enhance the public good is deflated by the ever-increasing environmental damage inflicted by externalities. As scientists learn more about their effects, the materials and processes of advanced industrialism loom more and more menacing to public health and worker life and safety.

2. WHAT IS THE FUTURE OF CAPITALISM?

Monetarism's total rejection of Keynesian economic policy and its outright, fundamentalist defence of capitalism make very clear to us the choice facing everyone of us today. What is the future of capitalism to be? Can we believe that monetarism's pursuit of the free market and non-interventionist government will lead to the rescue of capitalism, to prosperity — or to disaster? Or are we headed for an updated variation on Keynesian government planning?

Much as was the case half a century ago, in 1929, the world economy seems delicately poised at the top of a steep hill. Can market capitalism stand the strain of reduced growth and darkened prospects of rising living standards?

From the twin perspectives of economic justice and capitalist survival, enlightened responses to these interlinked challenges would be redistributive, alike within rich communities and between them and the impoverished losers of the Third World.

Early in 1980 the Brandt Commission issued an enlightened report which pleaded urgently the case for reformulation of relations between the First and the Third World. But rich countries evince little disposition to transfer the capital and technology necessary to accelerated development. If anything, the United States and Western Europe seem inclined to narrow access to their markets and reduce foreign aid.

The actual policies of the rich nations thus far combine continuation of economic imperialism abroad and increasing acceptance of monetarism at home.

John Maynard Keynes, son of a Cambridge academic family, mandarin of mandarins, intimate of Virginia Woolf's Bloomsbury, and, at his death, member of the House of Lords, imparted new impetus to capitalism, but only at the price of substantially modifying reliance on free markets. Keynes legitimized tax cuts and public spending in recession or depression. His emphasis upon aggregate demand as the means to economic growth and full employment justified on nonaltruistic grounds the welfare state's income maintenance provisions — pensions for the elderly, unemployment benefits for the jobless, and health and housing subsidies addressed to low income beneficiaries in particular.

As the Keynesian era waned in the late 1960s and the unravelling of economic policy accelerated in the early 1970s, it turned out that Keynesians had no solution to the stagflation of the decade.

The time was ripe for counter-revolution, the role enthusiastically embraced by Milton Friedman, son of impoverished Jewish immigrants, Nobel laureate, inventor of monetarism, apostle of capitalist freedom.

Capitalism may self-destruct, but a different scenario is more likely. Intelligent capitalist apologists realize that resumption of economic growth at 1960s rates is highly improbable.

Sophisticated capitalists are no less aware than John Kenneth Galbraith and his followers that modern capitalism is an affair of powerful institutions — giant corporations, national unions, foundations, health cartels, and governments. With the possible but vanishing exception of the United States, modern capitalism is strongly influenced by a powerful coterie of planners. In France and Japan, economic success in the last third of a century has been promoted by active cooperation and coordination between central government and major corporations or trading groups.

This is corporatism, explicit collaboration between big business, and, as a result, intensified wage earner subordination to the corporate sector. At the moment, most American businessmen and their media sympathizers oppose government intervention into so-called free markets. In fact, corporate leaders spend many of their waking hours on the hunt for tax benefits, loan guarantees, protection from foreign rivals, investment credits, and relaxation of regulatory restraints.

Even in America, prominent businessmen like Henry Ford II, Chase Manhattan's David Rockefeller, former Treasury Secretary W. Michael Blumenthal, Brown Brothers Harriman's Robert Roosa, and Lazard Frères' Felix Rohatyn have endorsed national economic planning. They seem intelligently reconciled to supporting limited social welfare benefits as the price of social stability and continued mass political apathy.

Some suspect that the arrangements for the rescue of New York City from bankruptcy in 1975, which gave the metropolis's bankers major influence over municipal budgets, limited the role of unions of public workers, and sharply reduced public and social services, amount to a trial run in corporate planning, a model for extension to the nation.

Even if the rational, sophisticated, planning wing of American business carries the day, capitalism's respite is likely to be temporary. Although corporate planners might well create a sensible energy policy, guide investment in general, and otherwise tidy up a disorderly economy, the resources available to them in a slowly growing economy will be too scant to generate profits satisfactory to investors, wages adequate to gratify even diminished worker expectations, and the social benefits of even a minimal welfare state.

More than an impulse, rather an urgent need, of corporatism, as of earlier stages of capitalism, is redistribution of income away from labour, toward property. Efforts to do so intensify the familiar Marxist contradiction between abundant supply and inadequate purchasing power. Looming crises of overproduction and declining rates of profit can no longer be resolved, after the fashion of the 19th century, by exploitation of an aroused Third World as a source of cheap raw materials and an outlet for excess inventories of finished goods. Indeed the scramble for markets is all but certain to increase the disarray of rich countries as multinationals, based in Europe, Japan, and the United States, clash and embroil their own governments.

What next? It may well occur that growing worker disaffection and increasing social tension will frighten dominant corporate and financial interests into an authoritarian response. It is easy to believe that business leaders, always far more attached to their own power and influence than to the mass forms of democracy, will, under stress, jettison civil liberties and parliamentary institutions. Whether a successor regime was one of the reactionary right or classically fascist might be a question more of linguistic taste than real difference.

There is a more attractive and not necessarily less possible alternative. The wage slaves of capitalism are no fools. In the United States, their past endorsement of private ownership and market capitalism registered satisfaction in their own material advancement. Even blacks, who have fared far worse than majority whites, preserved hopes of better lives for their sons and daughters.

All parties, black and white, male and female, are discovering that capitalism no longer delivers the rising living standards which in time past served as its major justification. Average citizens can no longer afford the luxury of abstaining from politics or treating contests for office as spectator sports. The self-interest of those who live by their labour requires replacement of capitalism by democratic socialism.

Bibliography

Classics

Keynes, J.M. **The General Theory of Employment, Interest and Money,**New York: Harcourt, Brace, 1936; MacMillan, London 1963. The great man's masterpiece is singularly opaque to the laity but redeemed by lightning flashes of eloquence.

Malthus, T.R. **An Essay on Population**, New York: Dutton, Everyman, 2 volumes, 1960-1; Everyman's University Library, London 1973. As an excuse for despair and a pretext for neglecting the poor, Malthus' population doctrine has had a long run by no means ended.

Marx, Karl, **Capital**, New York: International Publishers, 1967, 3 volumes; Lawrence and Wishart, London, 1970-72. Past the first, formidable 150 pages, Vol I is a burning indictment of 19th century capitalism and a passionate account of its origins. Vol II is mostly for specialists but much of Vol III remains accessible to the motivated.

Smith, Adam, **The Wealth of Nations**, New York: Modern Library, 1937; Everyman's Library, London,1977. Still fun to read and full of surprises, notably Smith's affection for the working class and distrust of capitalists.

Analysts and Prophets

Barnet, Richard J. and Muller, Ronald, E., **Global Reach**, New York: Simon & Schuster, 1974. An excellent, highly critical discourse on the role and menace of multinational corporations.

Friedman, Milton and Friedman, Rose, **Free to Choose**, New York: Harcourt Brace Jovanovich, 1980; Secker and Warburg, London, 1980. Adam Smith said it all better, earlier and funnier, but Friedman is a force in the world, more's the pity.

Galbraith, John Kenneth, **The New Industrial State**, Boston: Houghton Mifflin, 1971; Deutsch, London, 1972. The large corporation as a planning institution. The glorification of experts can be taken with a quantity of salt.

Gamble, Andrew "The Free Economy and the Strong State", **The Socialist Register 1979**, Merlin Press: London, 1979.

Hammond, John L. and Hammond, Barbara, **The Town Labourer**, New York: Longmans, Green, 1917; Longman, London 1972. Later economic historians assert that living standards rose during the Industrial Revolution. The Hammonds demonstrated how miserable life was for the ordinary worker in the grim new industrial communities.

Heilbroner, Robert L., **Beyond Boom and Crash**, New York: Norton, 1978; Marion Boyars, London 1979. A speculation that the increasing creakiness of capitalism will lead in the near future to right wing authoritarianism.

Lekachman, Robert, **The Age of Keynes**, New York: Random House, 1966; Allen Lane, London, 1967. An introduction to the man and his theory. Feel free to ignore the cheerful tone. Times have changed and the author has sensibly moved to the left.

Polanyi, Karl, **The Great Transformation**, New York: Farrar and Rinehart, 1944. A powerful argument that the human destruction caused by industrialization evoked early in the 19th century the beginnings of the welfare state.

Schumpeter, Joseph A., **Capitalism, Socialism and Democracy**, New York: Harper, 1942; Allen and Unwin, London, 1977. A highly original demonstration by an admirer of capitalism that the system's very success will lead to its supercession by socialism.

Sombart, Werner, **Why Is There No Socialism in the United States?** White Plains: International Arts and Sciences Press, 1976. No heritage of feudalism, the frontier spirit, and, above all, roast beef and apple pie. What happens when the beef is sliced thinner?

174

Other titles in Pantheon's documentary comic-book series:

Marx for Beginners

"I recommend it unreservedly for anyone who wants the rudiments of Marx from an engaging mentor."

Andrew Hacker, *New York Times*

The Anti-Nuclear Handbook

"This high-spirited, well-informed and unabashed work of propaganda is a morbidly amusing work to ponder while waiting for the neighborhood meltdown."
New York Times

Lenin for Beginners

"This book is documentary history at its most exciting and informative."
Washington Post

Freud for Beginners

"The treatment of Freud is rigorous, but watching it unfold is just plain fun."
In These Times

Einstein for Beginners

"This book is well-illustrated and thoroughly researched.…The presentation of [Einstein's] discoveries is little short of inspired."

Washington Post

Mao for Beginners

"Mao Tse-tung made history.…Now his works are finally accessible to the western masses."
UPI Book Corner

Trotsky for Beginners

"A quick, irreverent and rounded portrait.…Beginners will enjoy the book—and so will everyone else."

Charleston Evening Post